BAHA'I

FRANCIS BECKWITH

BETHANY HOUSE PUBLISHERS
MINNEAPOLIS, MINNESOTA 55438
A Division of Bethany Fellowship, Inc.

Dedication

To Harold and Elizabeth Beckwith of 4710 El Tesoro Avenue—the house with the basketball hoop on the side.

"Train a child in the way he should go, and when he is old he will not turn from it."

—Proverbs 22:6

Published by Bethany House Publishers
A Division of Bethany Fellowship, Inc.
6820 Auto Club Road, Minneapolis, Minnesota 55438

Printed in the United States of America

Library of Congress Cataloging in Publication Data

Beckwith, Francis.
  Baha'i.

  Bibliography: p.
  1. Bahai Faith—Controversial literature.   1. Title
BP370.B43   1985   239   85-20161
ISBN 0-87123-848-9

Table of Contents

PREFACE

In an age in which uncertainty is glorified and skepticism is a virtue, the serious discussion of religious truth has, more or less, become a tolerated vice—". . . blind men searching in dark rooms for non-existent black cats."[1] Though this type of thinking grips the spirit of our secular age, this author, like Socrates of old, will not succumb to popular opinion, as if it were an infallible barometer of all truth. History tells us that the masses have been mistaken before (i.e., remember the flat earth theory), and there is no reason to suppose that this age is history's grand exception. For this reason, this critique of Baha'ism is written with no apology. And our defense of Christianity is written with no shame.

In this book we plan to deal with two aspects of the Baha'i religion: (1) The main teachings of the faith (dogmatics); and (2) The Baha'i use of the Bible in defense of their religion (apologetics). In addition, this answers several questions concerning the relationship between Christianity and Baha'ism.

First, can we place the teachings of Jesus Christ into the Baha'i religion without any damage to the original intent and meaning of these teachings? Second, is the Baha'i use of the Bible successful, compelling, or legitimate? And third, does the Baha'i religion have objective evidence on which to rest its beliefs? Is Christianity any different in this respect? We intend to sufficiently answer these questions.

Acknowledgements

Special thanks to Lorraine Gerber for typing the original manuscript, and to Dr. Charles Manske for his constructive criticism and sound advice. In addition, special thanks to Uncle Stephen Guido for his unmerited kindness in allowing me free use of his computer in order to write the final draft.

Chapter 1

A HISTORY OF THE BAHA'I FAITH

The Baha'i faith is a relatively new religion, having begun about 140 years ago (1844) in Persia (Iran).[1] Though sometimes treated as a sect or cult of Islam (it originated out of Shi'ite Islam), Baha'ism should be considered an independent religion. Just as Buddhism originated within the context of Hinduism and Christianity within the framework of Judaism, but eventually were distinguished from their parent religion, so the Baha'i faith should now be considered distinct from Islam.[2]

> The Babis [Baha'is] are Muhammadans only in the sense that Muhammadans are Christians or the Christians Jews; that is to say, they recognize Muhammed (Mohomet) as a true prophet and the Qur'an (Koran) as a revelation, but they deny their finality.[3]

Though popularly known for its high moral standards, the Baha'i faith is much more. This religion has some definite beliefs concerning the nature of God, the nature of revelation, the nature of man, and the finality of the Baha'i religion itself.[4]

To caution us from considering the Baha'i faith a mere set of moral standards, Alessandro Bausani, a Baha'i himself, and Professor of Persian Literature and Islamistics at Rome University, writes:

> The Baha'i faith declares itself a religion. Though its doctrines are so simple that some have taken it for a philosophical or humanitarian movement, the history of its founding and its first historic period belies such an interpretation.[5]

The primary and basic Baha'i belief is that all religions derive from the same source. According to the Baha'i religion, in almost every era God has manifested himself in certain individuals. Moses, Zoroaster, Jesus, Muhammed, Krishna, Buddha, Confucius, the Bab, and Baha'u'llah were all prophets or manifestations of God in their times. However, Baha'u'llah, as the last and greatest of them all, should be revered and obeyed. Baha'u'llah's greatest teaching was the oneness and unity of mankind. According to Baha'u'llah, all races, both sexes, and all religious truths come from the work of one God.[6]

The Baha'i faith, indeed, is a religion which centers in devotion to a person believed to be God's manifestation for the modern age; it demands unreserved acceptance of his person as God's latest revelation to the world and requires absolute submission to his every word and command.[7]

The Ministry of the Bab (1844–1853) [8]

As stated earlier, the Baha'i faith originated out of the Islamic sect of the Shi'ites. This sect, especially in Persia, has always taught that Muhammed's son-in-law and legitimate successor, Ali, had twelve legitimate descendents. These twelve descendents (imams), often called "gates," were considered the means (a gate) by which a believer could have access to the true Faith. Since the disappearance of the twelfth successor in the ninth century A.D., it has been believed among the Shi'ites that he would some day reappear as a type of messiah.[9]

In 1844, declaring himself to be the twelfth *imam*, a Shi'ite named Mirza Ali Muhammed began calling himself the Bab. The Bab, with his followers (known as Babis), began to promote radical social and religious changes.[10] For instance, the Bab was a strong supporter of raising the status of women, a position contrary to Islamic teaching of his day. For example, the Bab taught that men were allowed to speak with women,[11] and that women, though still forbidden to go on pilgrimages, may go to the mosque at night for their devotions (IV, 18–19).[12] This does not sound like radical feminism today, but for Islamic society in the mid-nineteenth century, it was revolutionary.

The Bab's social and religious reforms included many other aspects that few Baha'is are familiar with. For instance, the Bab prohibited the study of law, logic, philosophy, dead languages, and grammar (IV, 10).[13] All Muslim books were to be destroyed, except the Qur'an (VI, 6).[14] The Bab also taught that kings who become Babis must seek to evangelize others and to remove unbelievers from their countries and jurisdictions (VII, 16; IX, 2).[15] However, in all fairness to the present day Baha'is, it must be stated that though they respect and believe him to be a divine manifestation like Buddha or Jesus, the Bab is no longer the current manifestation. Therefore, his pronouncements are no longer binding for today's follower of Baha'u'llah.

The Babi movement had a short life span. After much persecution of him and his followers, the Bab was publicly executed in 1850. However, prior to his death, the Bab predicted that he had prepared the way for one who would come after him and form a universal religion.[16]

The Ministry of Baha'u'llah (1853–1892)

An imprisoned disciple of the Bab, Mirza Husayn Ali, was a son of one of Persia's most distinguished families. Because of his family name, he avoided execution but was imprisoned in Tehran.[17]

Mirza Husayn was banished to Baghdad after one of the Bab's disciples tried to assassinate the Shah of Iran. This attempted assassination caused greater persecution for Mirza's followers. While imprisoned in Tehran, and during his ten-year exile in Baghdad, it became evident to Mirza that he was the one whom the Bab predicted would arrive.[18]

In 1863 the remaining Babis and Mirza were banished to Constantinople. On the evening before they journeyed, Mirza told the Babis that he was the one whom the Bab had foretold would come. After the declaration, Mirza took the name Baha'u'llah (the glory of God), and all the Babis who believed this declaration and obeyed Baha'u'llah's commands were known as Baha'is.[19]

After years of being dragged from one prison to another and being persecuted, Baha'u'llah and the Baha'is were banished to the prison city of 'Akka' in Israel. Though he was given more liberty as the years progressed, Baha'u'llah spent the rest of his life as a prisoner of the Turkish government in 'Akka.'[20]

Despite his prisoner status, Baha'u'llah spent his remaining days seeing guests, sending off missionaries, and writing books and letters. Among the books he wrote was his book of laws, the *Kitab-i-Agdas*. This is considered his "most weighty and sacred work."[21] Baha'u'llah wrote letters to the leaders of many nations, including the Roman Catholic Pope. In them he proclaimed his purpose. In 1892 he passed away in 'Akka' at the age of 75.[22]

The Ministries of 'Abdu'l-Baha' and Shoghi Effendi, and the Years that Followed

Abbas Effendi, the son of Baha'u'llah, who later became known as 'Abdu'l-Baha', had the religion's leadership passed on to him. Unlike his father or the Bab, 'Abdu'l-Baha' never claimed to be a manifestation of God. He was merely the leader of the faith who had the final word when it came to interpreting the meaning of Baha'u'llah's teachings. Like his father, 'Abdu'l-Baha' was a prolific writer and an awe inspiring speaker. After being released by the same Turkish government that imprisoned Baha'u'llah, 'Abdu'l-Baha' spent the remaining years of his life travelling throughout Europe and North America proselytizing potential new converts and forming Baha'i assemblies.[23]

In 1920 the British Empire bestowed knighthood upon 'Abdu'l-Baha'. He received this honor because of his work for world peace and unity. After 'Abdu'l-Baha' passed away in 1921, Baha'i leadership was placed in the hands of his grandson, Shoghi Effendi. Effendi continued to work for the furthering of the Baha'i faith.

After Effendi's death in 1957, the Baha'i people no longer were governed by a descendent of Baha'u'llah, but by an elected body of Baha'is representing all parts of the globe.[24] However, it should be noted that the transition from Effendi's leadership to the elected body of Baha'i representatives (the Universal House of Justice) did not go as smoothly as the Baha'is would like to depict it.

The disputes that arose after Effendi's death spawned the allegedly heretical Baha'i sect, *The Orthodox Baha'i Faith*. Organized by excommunicated Jason Remey, this sect differs little from the Baha'i World Faith in its doctrines concerning God's oneness and the unity of the major world religions. Its chief dispute with the main body concerns the line of leadership in the Baha'i community. Orthodox Baha'is deny that the Universal House of Justice is the proper successor of Shoghi Effendi. They believe that Mason Remey was Effendi's true successor.[25]

At the present time, the Baha'is, who have their international headquarters in Haifa, Israel, are suffering tremendous persecution in Iran.[26] In the United States the Baha'is have their national headquarters in Wilmette, Illinois. In Wilmette they have built an extremely beautiful nine-sided temple, which represents the nine great religious leaders of the world they believe are manifestations of the one God.

Chapter 2

A PRESENTATION OF BAHA'I DOGMATICS

The Baha'i Doctrine of God

The Unknowability of God

The Baha'is teach that God is an unknowable essence. According to 'Abdu'l-Baha', "the Reality of the Divinity is hidden from all comprehension, and concealed from the minds of all men. It is absolutely impossible to ascend to that plane."[1] Baha'u'llah writes:

> To every discerning and illuminated heart it is evident that God, the unknowable Essence, the Divine Being, is immensely exalted beyond every human attribute, such as corporeal existence, ascent and descent, egress and regress. Far be it from His glory that the tongue should adequately recount His praise, or that the human heart comprehend the fathomless mystery. He is, and hath ever been, veiled in the ancient eternity of His Essence, and remains in His Reality everlastingly hidden from the sight of men.[2]

However, the question that immediately arises is: If the Baha'is believe in a God, how do they know anything about His existence if nothing can be known about His essence?

In response to this question 'Abdu'l-Baha' states that God, "this Essence of essences, this Truth of truths, this mystery of mysteries," may "reveal" something of Himself through "reflections, auroras, appearances and resplendencies, in the world of existence." According to 'Abdu'l-Baha', one of the ways God does reveal Himself is through His manifestations.[3]

> All the perfections, the bounties, the spleandors which come from God, are visible and evident in the Reality of the Holy Manifestations, like the sun which is resplendent in a clear polished mirror with all its perfections and bounties.[4]

> Therefore all that the human reality knows, discovers, and understands of the names, the attributes, and the perfection of God, refer to these Holy Manifestations. There is no access to anything else: "the way is closed and seeking is forbidden."[5]

For the contemporary Baha'i, God is known only through and by individuals known as manifestations. "By the revelation of these" manifestations "all the names and attributes of God, such as knowledge and power, sovereignty and dominion, mercy and wisdom, glory, bounty, and grace, are manifest."[6]

The Baha'i Doctrines of Revelation and Manifestations

According to Baha'i doctrine, *revelation* is a continuous process. There is no final, complete or finished word of God. This position is put forth rather well by Shoghi Effendi, who writes:

> The fundamental principle enunciated by Baha'u'llah, the followers of His Faith believe, is that religious truth is not absolute, but relative, that Divine Revelation is a continuous and progressive process, that all the great religions of the world are divine in origin, that their basic principles are in complete harmony, that their aims and purposes are one and the same, that their teachings are but facets of one truth, that their functions are complimentary, that they differ only in non-essential aspects of their doctrines, and that their missions represent successive stages in the spiritual evolution of human society.[7]

In Baha'i doctrine, whenever there are beliefs that are held in common by all the major world religions, unity is found. Whenever the Baha'is find contradictory material that is somewhat reconcilable, then a sense of unity is achieved. However, when doctrinal differences create a barrier, they are considered unimportant. In this way, Baha'i doctrine is preserved from any type of criticism concerning contradictions between any of the so-called progressive revelations. One must realize that to be preserved from criticism is a two-edged sword. For one is also as equally preserved from proof. This absence of accountability is the type of protection that strips any religion of its proof and renders its pronouncements meaningless. For example, if you were told that there existed a planet a little bit farther out than Pluto, which no telescope could detect, what would you think of that opinion? Sure, one could boast that it cannot be disproved. However, what good would that do? This theory, though invincible to criticism, is unprovable and therefore worthless.

According to Baha'i doctrine, whenever God gives a revelation in a particular era of human history, He does it through His manifestations. They bring new laws and revelations that would have been too difficult for the people of previous dispensations to comprehend or understand.[8] Townshend writes:

> The High-Prophet himself, though he endorses all the spiritual teachings of the last Revelation, does not hesitate to modify or repeal the material regulations and the ceremonies enjoined by his predecessors. These were given to the minds of the people at a particular stage of their growth. But in a continuously changing world, rites and rules which are expedient today will not be so tomorrow.[9]

The manifestation may change insignificant ordinances of the previous manifestations, such as modes of worship, rules about fasts and feasts, drinking, marriage, and eating, but he never changes *eternal truths*.[10] Some of the eternal truths have been put forth by Baha'i, Gloria Faizi, who writes:

> Despite the great conflict of ideas that now exists among people professing different Faiths, there are certain essential similarities between the major religions of the past which are too obvious to be overlooked. They all believe in a Creator, whether they call him God, the First Cause, or some other name. They all have a central figure— one lone Man—Whose love has changed the lives of millions of people and whose words are still a source of hope and inspiration many centuries after they were spoken. They all promise that in time, when men have lost faith and love has grown cold, a Great One will appear to gather the children of men from the four corners of the earth and usher in the day of universal Brotherhood.[11]

Concerning a manifestation's position in his particular dispensation, Townshend writes:

> His precepts and ordinances are to be obeyed as from God; his teaching is sufficient for salvation; none approach God save through him, since in him alone God is manifest and to turn from him is to turn from God. However unworthy the people . . . his work cannot fail nor his mission go unaccomplished.[12]

Since there have been innummerable religious movements and leaders in history, how does the Baha'i religion distinguish between a true manifestation and a false one? In order to solve this problem, several Baha'i writers have put forth some criteria. The following is a list of the chief criteria found in Baha'i literature:

(1) His Truth Is Self-Validating

> . . .His manifestation can adduce no greater proof of the truth of His mission than the proof of His own person.[13]

(2) He Fulfills Prophecy and Foretells His Successor

> Thus does every High-Prophet on his appearance draw attention as part of his credentials, to his fulfillment of authentic prediction; and before he departs, he foretells the continuance of the prophetic line.[14]

(3) Each Manifestation Is a Different Individual

> Whether a High-Prophet in giving his accustomed prediction says: "I will come again," or "Another like me will come," his meaning is the same, and his purpose is in both cases to bear witness to the continuity of revelation. It is not recorded in any prophetic line that the same individual (the same mother's son) ever returned to earth to carry on his own work. . .[15]

(4) There Is an Appointed Time of Successions

> Each takes the work from the hand of his predecessor and carries it forward at the appointed hour he resigns his completed work to his own successors.[16]

(5) He Is Humble, Uneducated, and Has No Status

> As a man, he is marked by his simplicity and gentleness and lack of personal

ambition. Often he is born of lowly parents, is obscure and impecunious. He is always a man of little human learning. [17]

(6) The Manifestation Is Sinless

For these Holy Souls are pure from every sin, and sanctified from faults. [18]

(7) He Manifests Extraordinary Ethical Attributes

These divine Messengers manifest in their own lives attributes of God, such as love, mercy, justice, and power, to a degree far above the capacity of ordinary human beings. [19]

(8) He Brings a New Name and a New Attribute of God

The High-Prophet brings always a new Name of God—not only a new title but a new attribute; that is, he admits into the human consciousness a new attribute by which God is realized, a fuller conception of God. [20]

(9) He Brings Harmony Among People

A new basis of agreement is realized among men, and people long sundered by prejudice of race and class find themselves united by strong bands of harmony and affection. [21]

(10) He Changes Hearts, Not Using External Power

He changes the hearts of men and the economy of nations by quickening the process of growth rather than by external display of power; and the results of his influence do not appear immediately. [22]

Now let us look more closely at the individuals the Baha'i Faith considers to be the manifestations of God. In 1908, 'Abdu'l-Baha' said that the manifestations of God were Abraham, Moses, Christ, Muhammed, the Bab, and Baha'u'llah. [23] In October 1912 he said the manifestations of God were Moses, Jesus, Zoroaster, Krishna, Buddha, Confucius, and Muhammed, in addition to the Bab and Baha'u'llah. [24] The Bab, who preceded Baha'u'llah and 'Abdu'l-Baha', includes Adam as one of the manifestations. [25] Baha'u'llah said that the manifestations were Noah, Hud, [26] Salih, [27] Abraham, Moses, Jesus, Muhammed, and the Bab. [28] According to another list, the nine revealed religions of the world are the Sabean religion, Hinduism, Judaism, Zoroastrianism, Buddhism, Christianity, Islam, the Babi religion, and the Baha'i religion. [29] However, according to Hugh E. Chance, the nine religions recognized by the Baha'is are Hinduism, Zoroastrianism, Buddhism, Confucianism, Taoism, Judaism, Christianity, and the Baha'i religion. [30]

Nevertheless, when all is said and done, the authoritative sources of the Babi-Baha'i religion have, at one time or another, recognized the following as legitimate manifestations of God: Adam, Noah, Abraham, Moses, Krishna, Zoroaster, Jesus, Buddha, Confucius, Muhammed, Hud, Salih, the Bab, and Baha'u'llah. Though the Baha'i religion presently mentions only nine of the above manifestations, they have never denied the recognition of the others.

For such a denial to occur, it would mean that the Baha'i Faith would have to contradict its own self-admitted authorities. This can never happen.

BAHA'ISM AND JESUS CHRIST

To conclude our study in Bahai's major teachings, we will examine the Baha'i view of Jesus Christ. Traditionally, in Christian theology and in the New Testament, Jesus Christ has been said to possess several distinguishing characteristics that have set Him apart from all other human beings. Four of these unique characteristics are the following: (1) He is God Incarnate; (2) He will return in the skies in bodily form; (3) He rose bodily from the grave; (4) He is the only Savior of mankind for all eternity. We will examine each one of these individually. (See chapter 3 for a more thorough Christian response to the Baha'is' position on these points.)

Jesus Christ Is God Incarnate

Christians have believed for centuries that Jesus Christ is God come in the flesh. However, according to Baha'i doctrine, the Christian church has been mistaken. Baha'u'llah writes:

> Know thou of a certainty that the Unseen can in no wise incarnate His Essence and reveal it unto men.[31]

In other words, it is not that God *did* not incarnate Himself, but rather, that He *could* not. Denial of the Incarnation is also put forth by 'Abdu'l-Baha', who writes in his essay on the Trinity, that "for God to descend into the conditions of existence would be the greatest of imperfections."[32] In addition, he writes:

> Was Christ within God, or God within Christ? No, in the name of God![33]

The Baha'i religion teaches that Jesus Christ is one of several manifestations of God; they flatly deny the Christian doctrine of the Incarnation. According to the Baha'is, a manifestation is merely a reflection of God's essence,[34] while an incarnation is God's essence made flesh.[35] This distinction is extremely important.

Jesus Christ Will Return in the Skies in Bodily Form

A second primary doctrine denied by the Baha'is is the Second Coming of Christ. Though Baha'is claim that they believe this doctrine, they actually do not. What they believe is that Baha'u'llah, as God's manifestation for this dispensation, is Christ returned.[36] The Baha'is attempt to justify this dogma by citing specific Biblical prophecies that appear to have been fulfilled in the person of Baha'u'llah.[37] Concerning the Second Coming of Christ, 'Abdu'l-Baha' writes:

> At the first coming he came from heaven, though apparently from the womb; in the same way also, at his second coming, he will come from heaven, though apparently from the womb.[38]

It is obvious that the Baha'i faith denies the traditional Christian belief concerning the return of Jesus Christ in the skies in bodily form.

Jesus Christ Rose Bodily From the Grave

The Baha'i faith denies the long-held Christian doctrine that Jesus rose bodily from the grave. 'Abdu'l-Baha', after being questioned as to the meaning and significance of Christ's Resurrection, responded as follows:

> The resurrections of Divine Manifestations are not of the body . . . his resurrection from the interior of the earth is also symbolic; it is a spiritual and divine fact; and likewise his ascension to heaven is a spiritual and not material ascension.[39]

He continues:

> Therefore we say that the meaning of Christ's resurrection is as follows: The disciples were troubled and agitated by the martyrdom of Christ. The Reality of Christ, which signifies his teachings, his bounties, his perfections, and his spiritual power, was hidden and concealed for two or three days after his martyrdom, and was not resplendent and manifest. No, rather it was lost; for the believers were few in number and were troubled and agitated. The Cause of Christ was like a life-less body; and, when after three days the disciples became assured and steadfast, and began to serve the Cause of Christ, and resolved to spread the divine teachings, putting his counsels into practice, and arising to serve him, the Reality of Christ became resplendent and his bounty appeared; his religion found life, his teachings and his admonitions became evident and visible.[40]

Simply stated, the Baha'is explain the accounts of Christ's Resurrection as merely symbolic or spiritual. For the Baha'i faith, it was His words and teachings, not the resurrected Christ, which gave the Early Church the needed power to evangelize and radically transform the Roman Empire.

Jesus Christ Is the Only Savior for All Eternity

The Christian doctrine that Jesus is "the way, the truth, and the life" for all time, is denied by the Baha'i doctrine of divine manifestations. The Baha'is teach that after six hundred years of Christianity, God saw fit to replace Jesus with Muhammed as the divine manifestation. Thus, a new dispensation began, and the position of Jesus as the only way to God was no longer in effect. Townshend writes:

> The advent of a Divine Messenger does not seem to be represented in the canon or the sacred writings of any world religion, as is surely not represented in the Christian Scripture, as an isolated phenomenon, simply an angelic adventure; nor is the Messenger shown as a solitary figure. He comes expressly as one of a line of teachers and is sent on a specific mission. He appears invariably in fulfillment of an ancient authoritative promise.[41]

In light of the above quote, and the fact that Baha'ism teaches that none of the manifestations "affirmed his revelation was final or exhaustive,"[42] it is rather obvious that Baha'ism flatly denies the uniqueness of Jesus Christ.

CONCLUSION

To capsulize what we have gone over in Baha'i teachings, the following should suffice. According to Baha'i dogmatics, man, by his own power, mental capacities, etc., cannot comprehend or know God. Therefore, because of this lack in man's make-up, God chose to reveal Himself through particular individuals known as divine manifestations. God is an unknowable essence, revealing particular attributes of Himself in each manifestation, with no manifestation being the final or last revelation of God.

According to the Baha'is, Jesus Christ, in contrast to what has been historically taught by the Christian Church and the New Testament, did not rise from the dead in the same body that hung on the cross, will not return in the clouds in bodily form, is not God Incarnate, and is not the only way by which all people must be saved.

Chapter 3

A CRITIQUE OF BAHA'I DOGMATICS

The following areas will be covered in this critique: (1) The Baha'i doctrine of God; (2) The Baha'i doctrines of revelation and manifestations; and (3) Baha'ism and Jesus Christ.

A CRITIQUE OF THE BAHA'I DOCTRINE OF GOD

Man, by his own power cannot comprehend or know God, according to Baha'i doctrine. He chooses to reveal Himself only through His manifestations. It is not contrary to Christian doctrine to say that we can only know God if He chooses to reveal Himself, but it is ironic that the Baha'i religion should teach this also. For when one examines the doctrine of God's nature, as revealed by the so-called manifestations, there exists a mass of contradictory doctrine.

God's Nature As Revealed by the Manifestations

The following is a breakdown of the nature of God, as taught by seven of the religious leaders who are considered manifestations by the Baha'i faith.

Moses (c. 1200 B.C.) believed in the existence of one personal God who was the Creator of the universe. According to Deut. 6:4, Moses said, "Hear, O Israel: The LORD our God, the LORD is one." Thus he affirmed the Judaic doctrine of Yahweh being the one and only God.

Krishna (c. 850–650 B.C.) taught that many gods existed:

By sacrifice shalt thou honour the gods and the gods will then love thee. . . For pleased with thy sacrifice, the gods will grant to thee the joy of all thy desires. [1]

Krishna also taught that everything is part of the Supreme Being, Brahman:

He is invisible: he cannot be seen. He is far and he is near, he moves and he moves not, but is within all and outside all. He is ONE in all, but seems as if he were many. He supports all beings: from him comes destruction, and from him comes creation.

When a man sees that the infinity of various beings is abiding in the ONE, and is an evolution from the ONE, then he becomes one with Brahman.[2]

Krishna also claimed to be an incarnation (avatar) of the Hindu god, Vishnu.[3] So for Krishna, many gods exist (polytheism), but are in reality, along with all existence, part of the Supreme Being, Brahman (pantheism).

Zoroaster (c. 700–600 B.C.) taught that there is a good Supreme Being named Ahura Mazda,[4] and an evil Supreme Being named Angra Mainyu. Though "the particular name 'Angra Mainyu,' as designating the supreme hostile spirit, occurs only once in the teachings of Zoroaster," the passage explicitly states "that from the beginning of existence there have been two inherently incompatible, antagonistic spirits in the world (Yasha 45:2)."[5]

Siddhartha Gautama (560–480 B.C.), better known as the Buddha, "did not teach a personal deity, worship or prayer."[6]

There is no category for God . . . because there is no doctrine of God in Buddhism. The Western theist must not expect a figure like the God of the Bible or the Qur'an in the religion of Buddha.[7]

Though in contemporary times there are many divisions of Buddhism that deify the Buddha or other beings (Bodhisattvas), the original teachings of the Buddha do not present God as a relevant topic.[8]

Confucius (c. 551–479 B.C.) was a polytheist who believed that the need for social order was more important than reverence for the gods. Writes Lewis Hopfe:

Confucius seems to have believed that, while the gods existed and worship and rituals were of value in bringing people together, these things were of secondary importance when compared to an equitable social order.[9]

Jesus Christ (4 B.C.—A.D. 29) taught that God was personal (Luke 23:34), transcendent (John 4:24), and that He Himself was an incarnation of this God (John 8:58 cf. Exodus 3:14). Jesus taught an essentially Judaic concept of God: a strict, uncompromising monotheism.

Muhammed (A.D. 570–632) taught a strict monotheism,[10] but denied that God could have a son through impregnating a woman (Qur'an 2:110; 4:169; 5:76–77; 6:100–102). This, of course, conflicts with Christ's claim to be the Son of God (John 5:18–19), and the New Testament account of His conception (Luke 1).

God and the Major World Religious Leaders

Religious Leader	Conception of god or gods
Moses	God is personal. Strict, uncompromising monotheism.
Krishna	Polytheistic, but ultimately pantheistic and impersonal.
Zoroaster	Two Supreme Beings. Philosophical dualism.
Buddha	God not relevant. Essentially agnostic.
Confucius	Polytheistic.
Jesus Christ	God is personal, able to beget a son. Strict, uncompromising monotheism.

| Muhammed | God is personal, unable to beget a son. Strict, uncompromising monotheism. |

There appears to be a confusion about God's nature among the alleged manifestations. Though Shoghi Effendi has said that the manifestations disagree on "non-essential aspects of their doctrine,"[11] it would stretch credibility to the limit to suppose that the nature of God is one of these non-essential aspects. God cannot be impersonal, personal, transcendent, polytheistic, pantheistic, monotheistic, able to beget, not able to beget, relevant, and irrelevant all at the same time. If it is true that God is all those things, then we are driven to agnosticism. Such an illogical God can never be known based on the contradictory information given to us by His alleged manifestations. Irreconcilable data gives us no knowledge of God whatsoever.

The Criteria for Manifestations

We must reject the criteria for manifestations set up by certain Baha'i apologists, because some of the manifestations do not fit the criteria they're supposed to live up to. For instance, George Townshend writes that the "High-Prophet himself, though he endorses all the spiritual teachings of the last Revelation, does not hesitate to modify or repeal. . ."[12]

It is noteworthy that Jesus, Confucius, Buddha, Zoroaster, and Krishna fail this test. Confucius, who was the manifestation prior to Christ, is never mentioned by Jesus. The Buddha, who came before Confucius (though historically his contemporary), is never found in the works of Confucius. The Buddha makes no reference to his predecessor, Zoroaster. Krishna, the manifestation preceding Zoroaster, is not mentioned by the Persian prophet. In addition, Krishna fails to talk of his predecessor, Moses.

Townshend sets forth another faulty criterion:

> As a man, he is marked by his simplicity and gentleness and lack of personal ambition. . . He is always a man of little human learning.[13]

This is not true of either Moses or Confucius. Concerning Moses, Josh McDowell and Don Stewart write:

> It must be initially stated that Moses was in a position to write the Pentateuch. He was educated in the royal court of Egypt, which was highly advanced academically.[14]

Concerning himself, Confucius said that at "fifteen I had my mind bent on learning."[15] Confucius was a successful teacher, and started a private school which grew till he had 3,000 students.

> He had varied interests and subjects of teaching: history, poetry, literature, properties, government, natural science, music.[16]

'Abdu'l-Baha' writes another invalid criterion of the manifestations: "For these Holy Souls are pure from every sin, and sanctified from faults."[17] Adam, Moses, Noah, Confucius, and Muhammed have all failed to live up to this standard. According to the first three chapters of Genesis, Adam committed a sinful act. He disobeyed the specific command of God not to eat from the tree of knowledge. His disobedience, and that of his mate, caused both to be banished from the Garden of Eden.

According to the second chapter of Exodus, Moses was guilty of murdering an Egyptian. The ninth chapter of Genesis records that Noah became drunk with wine. In his Analects, Confucius confesses specific moral shortcomings (7:3). He had hoped he would improve, "if only he could have fifty more years for study (7:16)."[18]

> The Master said: "In letters I am perhaps equal to other men. But the character of the superior man, carrying out in his conduct what he professes, is what I have not yet attained to." (7:32)[19]

He admitted being unable "not to be overcome with wine," and defective in four duties (9:15).[20]

It is said of Muhammed in the Qur'an (48:1–2):

> Lo! We have given thee (O Muhammed) a signal victory, That Allah may forgive thee of thy sin that which is past and that which is to come, and may perfect His favour unto thee, and may guide thee on a right path.[21]

In order to escape the fact that some of the manifestations were sinners, 'Abdu'l-Baha' has said:

> How often the Prophets of God and His universal Manifestations in their prayers confess their sins and faults! This is only to teach other men, to encourage and incite them to humility and weakness, and induce them to confess their sins and faults.[22]

Since none of the texts that have been presented support 'Abdu'l-Baha's interpretation, there is no reason to suppose his interpretation correct. 'Abdu'l-Baha's hermeneutic (rule of interpretation) has nothing to do with the evidence within a given text, but is an unjustified presupposition. In order to be fair to any world religious leader, one should accept what the leader says at face value, instead of twisting it in order to fit a predetermined belief. In other words, if the leader says, "I am a sinner," or "I have failed God," this must be accepted. It should not be distorted in order to fit a particular prejudice of the reader (such in the case of 'Abdu'l-Baha'—"the manifestations never sin."). The burden of proof is on the Baha'i leaders to justify their interpretation. Since they have not done so, we must accept what has been written at face value. This is the only honest and fair way to read any given text.

It could be said, without fear of contradiction, that the religious leaders who the Baha'i faith believes to be manifestations, are "authorities" with wax noses—noses which can be twisted in any way the Baha'i apologist sees fit, in order to keep his religious beliefs "consistent." In order to help the reader understand how an unjustified presupposition can harm one's thinking (as in the case of the Baha'i apologist), Dr. John Warwick Montgomery, Dean of the Simon Greenleaf School of Law, relates the following parable:

> Once upon a time (note the mystical cast) there was a man who thought he was dead. His concerned wife and friends sent him to the friendly neigh-

borhood psychiatrist. The psychiatrist determined to cure him by convincing him of one fact that contradicted his belief that he was dead. The fact the psychiatrist decided to use was the simple truth that dead men do not bleed. He put his patient to work reading medical texts, observing autopsies, etc. After weeks of effort the patient finally said, "All right, all right! You've convinced me! Dead men do not bleed." Whereupon the psychiatrist stuck him in the arm with a needle, and the blood flowed. The man looked down with a contorted ashen face and cried: "Good Lord! Dead men do bleed after all!"[23]

Another criterion, according to Townshend, is that the manifestation "changes the hearts of men . . . by quickening the process of growth rather than by external display of power."[24]

Jesus Christ does not fit this particular category. When asked by the Jews, "What miraculous sign can you show us to prove your authority to do all this?" (John 2:18), Jesus responded by saying, "Destroy this temple, and I will raise it again in three days" (John 2:19). John writes that Jesus was talking of the temple of His body (2:27). According to the accounts in Matthew, Mark, Luke, and John, the Resurrection was an external display of power, which quickened the hearts of the Apostles. Peter, the man who denied Jesus three times prior to the Resurrection (Luke 22:55–62), was able to say the following before a huge mob:

Men of Israel, listen to this: Jesus of Nazareth was a man accredited by God to you by miracles, wonders and signs, which God did among you through him, as you yourselves know. This man was handed over to you by God's set purpose and foreknowledge; and you, with the help of wicked men, put him to death by nailing him to the cross. (Acts 2:22–23)

The Apostle Paul writes:

And if Christ has not been raised, our preaching is useless and so is your faith. (1 Cor. 15:14)

In addition, the Apostle writes:

I want to know Christ and the power of his resurrection and the fellowship of sharing in his sufferings, becoming like him in his death. . . (Phil. 3:10)

It is obvious that Christianity rests on the power of the Resurrection. It is the external power of Christ's Resurrection that has quickened the internal lives of many. This is the testimony of the New Testament.

Baha'i Doctrine of Relative Revelation

For the Baha'i faith, there is no final, complete or finished Word of God. "The fundamental principle enunciated by Baha'u'llah . . . is that religious truth is not absolute, but relative. . . "[25] The problem with this concept of revelation is that it is self-defeating. The statement, "revelation is relative," which is allegedly a revelation spoken by Baha'u'llah, must be either relative or absolute. If the statement is relative, it is not absolutely binding, and it is possible that absolute revelation does exist. If the statement, "revelation is relative," is absolute, then the statement, "revelation is relative," cannot be true. Thus, the Baha'i doctrine of relative revelation is self-defeating and untrue.

However, a distinction must be made between *progressive* and *relative* revelation. The Christian faith teaches that God has *progressively* revealed Himself in particular books, culminating in the ultimate revelation of God, Jesus Christ (Heb. 1:1–2). Jesus verified His status as God Incarnate by rising from the dead (see Chapter 5). As God Incarnate, Jesus said that the books from Genesis to Malachi (the Old Testament) are the Word of God (Luke 24:27, 44). He taught that His teachings, which included the doctrine of Him being the only way to God, should be preached until the end of the world (Matthew 28:20).

BAHA'ISM AND JESUS CHRIST

The Baha'i faith denies the chief characteristics attributed to Christ. This denial can be answered by citing specific New Testament passages which contradict the Baha'i position. Baha'i representatives, such as Gloria Faizi, have said that "much of the Teachings of the Founders [Jesus in this case] is completely lost," and that "it is impossible to go back to their pure source and disentangle the original Message from the interpretation of its followers."[26] Since Ms. Faizi and other members of the Baha'i faith have yet to produce manuscripts or evidence to contradict or eradicate the words of Christ contained in the New Testament, and in light of the historical accuracy of the New Testament,[27] we have no choice but to appeal to the text now in our possession.

Jesus Christ Is God Incarnate

According to Baha'i doctrine, God *cannot* incarnate Himself.[28] This poses a rather peculiar problem. Though it is certainly possible that God *did* not or *will* not incarnate Himself, it is quite impossible, according to the Baha'i definition of God as an all-powerful Being,[29] for Him to be *unable* to incarnate Himself. God may be unwilling, but He cannot be unable.

After a careful examination of the New Testament, the reader becomes aware that Jesus and the biblical writers taught the doctrine of Incarnation. Several passages serve to demonstrate this.

In John 8:56–59, Jesus says to the Pharisees: " 'Your father Abraham rejoiced at the thought of seeing my day; he saw it and was glad.' 'You are not yet fifty years old,' the Jews said to him, 'and you have seen Abraham!' 'I tell you the truth,' Jesus answered, 'before Abraham was born, I am!' At this, they then picked up stones to stone him."

The term *I am*, as used in John 8:58, is the same term used by God while speaking of Himself in Ex. 3:14:

> God said to Moses, "I am who I am. This is what you are to say to the Israelites: 'I AM has sent me to you.' "

It is obvious, by the response of the Pharisees (the attempted stoning), that it was understood that Jesus claimed to be God. This is further supported by John 10:33, which reads:

> "We are not stoning you for any of these," replied the Jews, "but for blasphemy, because you, a mere man, claim to be God."

According to Hebrew law, there are only five cases that demand stoning: (1) Familiar spirits, Lev. 20:27; (2) Cursing (Blasphemy), Lev. 24:20–23; (3) False prophets who lead to idolatry, Deut. 13:5–10; (4) Stubborn son, Deut. 21:18–21; and (5) Adultery and rape, Deut. 22:21–24 and Lev. 20:10.[30] Walter R. Martin writes:

> Now any honest Biblical student must admit that the only legal ground the Jews had for stoning Christ (and actually they had none at all) was the second violation—namely, blasphemy.[31]

Further confirmation that Jesus referred to Himself as God in John 8:56–59, can be seen by an examination of the original language of the New Testament, Koine Greek. The emphatic term for *I am*, in the Greek, is rendered *ego eimi* (εγω ειμι).[32] The Septuagint, the Greek translation of the Hebrew Old Testament, renders God's *I am* statement in Ex. 3:14 as *ego eimi*.[33] It is obvious that Jesus, in John 8:56–59, claimed to be God Incarnate.

In Mark 2:5–7 Jesus claimed to be God when He forgave sins, an ability belonging only to God according to the Old Testament (Job 14:4; Ps. 130:4; Is. 43:25). This was easily recognized by the Jewish Pharisees, who said:

> Why does this fellow talk like that? He's blaspheming! Who can forgive sins but God alone? (Mark 2:7)

The Apostle Thomas, infamous for his doubting, called Jesus God. According to Christ, those who believe this doctrine, are blessed of God. The text reads:

> Thomas said to him, "My Lord and my God!" Then Jesus told him, "Because you have seen me, you have believed; blessed are those who have not seen and yet have believed." (John 20:28–29)

John, the man who penned Christ's claim to Deity in John 8:58, and who was an eyewitness to His life, understood the claims of Jesus very well. John writes:

> In the beginning was the Word, and the Word was with God, and the Word was God. . . The Word became flesh and lived for a while among us. We have seen his glory, the glory of the one and only Son, who came from the Father, full of grace and truth. (John 1:1,14)

John's proximity to the events and claims in question leaves 19th or 20th century reinterpretations of these claims much to be desired.

The Apostle Paul, whose writings and teachings were called Scripture by Simon Peter (2 Pet. 3:15–16—Peter knew Christ personally), writes, referring to Jesus: "For in Christ all the fullness of the Deity lives in bodily form. . ." (Col. 2:9). Paul taught the doctrine of the Incarnation.

Though many other Scriptural references can be cited to verify the doctrine of the Incarnation, the above citations are sufficient.[34]

In order to avoid the impact of the passages that clearly demonstrate Christ's Deity, the Baha'i faith has put forth a type of theological escape clause. It reads:

> Were any of the all-embracing Manifestations of God to declare: "I am God," He, verily, speaketh the truth, and no doubt attacheth thereto. [35]

However, Baha'u'llah continues:

> For it hath been repeatedly demonstrated that through their Revelation, their attributes and names, the Revelation of God, His names and His attributes, are manifest in the world. [36]

In other words, though Jesus claimed to be God, He really didn't mean it. According to the Baha'is, Christ's claims merely refer to the attributes of God manifested through His person, not to any incarnation. The problem with this form of reasoning is that it ignores the content of any passage that the Christian presents. Nowhere in the New Testament does Christ, the Apostles, or the writers of the New Testament, qualify the Incarnation in the Baha'i fashion. The Baha'i faith has set up a presupposition designed to squash any facts that appear to conflict with their own recognized dogma. (Remember the story of the man who thought he was dead?) The burden of proof rests on the Baha'i apologists to justify Baha'u'llah's presupposition of investigation. Since this has not been accomplished as of yet, we have little choice but to accept the text of the New Testament on its own merit.

Jesus Christ Will Return in the Skies in Bodily Form

In reference to Christ's Second Coming, and the biblical passages that mention it, the Baha'is fall into the same error as they do when they explain Christ's claims to Godhood. The Baha'i investigator, before examining any biblical text, begins with this presupposition:

> The second coming of Christ will be in like manner: the signs and conditions which have been spoken of all have meanings, and are not to be taken literally. [37]

In other words, no passage could ever convince a Baha'i that Christ will come again in bodily form in the skies. His presupposition has prevented him from investigating any facts on the matter. This is extremely unscientific, which, paradoxically, is one thing the Baha'is claim they are not. They boast of the essential unity of science and religion, [38] but they fail to practice this when investigating the Bible.

Some Baha'i apologists cite the fact that the Bible says Christ would come as a "thief in the night." [39] Thus, implying that "as a thief enters stealthily at night and is in the house while the master sleeps and knows it not, so he would come into a world wrapt in spiritual ignorance and would not be observed by those to whom he came." [40] However, when one reads the passages in question (Matt. 24:42–44; 1 Thessalonians 5:2,4), it is obvious that they are referring to the surprise factor of Christ's Second Coming, not to its secrecy or hiddenness. Matt. 24:42–44 reads:

Therefore keep watch, because you do not know on what day your Lord will come. But understand this: If the owner of the house had known at what time of night the thief was coming, he would. . . not have let his house be broken into. So you also must be ready, because the Son of Man will come at an hour when you do not expect him.

Paul writes in 1 Thess. 5:2, 4:

. . . for you know very well that the day of the Lord will come like a thief in the night. . . But you, brothers, are not in darkness so that this day should surprise you like a thief.

However, 'Abdu'l-Baha' has written that Christ's return will be like His first coming (being born as an infant).[41] Do the Scriptures tell us otherwise? Luke records, in Acts 1:9–11, the Ascension of Jesus. It reads:

After he said this, he was taken up before their very eyes, and a cloud hid him from their sight. They were looking intently up into the sky as he was going, when suddenly two men dressed in white stood beside them. "Men of Galilee," they said, "why do you stand here looking into the sky? This same Jesus, who has been taken from you into heaven, will come back in the same way you have seen him go into heaven."

Taken on its own merit, apart from any Baha'i presupposition (non-literalism), it is crystal clear that the above passage is claiming that Christ will return the same way He left. He departed via the sky, therefore, He will return that way.

The Baha'i faith claims that Baha'u'llah is Christ returned. They use many biblical passages in attempting to demonstrate this.[42] To Baha'u'llah's misfortune, however, he has failed the criterion of returning in the skies. He also failed the test of Rev. 1:7, which reads: "Look, he is coming with the clouds, and every eye will see him. . . ."

Baha'u'llah was not seen by every eye, and is therefore not the return of Christ. The Baha'is may attempt to explain away Rev. 1:7 by saying that the word *eye* does not refer to a literal eye, but rather, to an inward eye of understanding, as the Jehovah Witnesses have argued. However, an examination of the Greek word for eye in the passage, *ophthalmos* (ὀφθαλμὸς), renders the argument meaningless. The same Greek word used for the natural eye in Matt. 20:33, *ophthalmoi*, is used by John in Rev. 1:7.[43] Matt. 24:30, another passage which teaches the literal return of Christ, has this to say:

At that time the sign of the Son of Man will appear in the sky, and all the nations of the earth will mourn. They will see the Son of Man coming on the clouds of the sky, with power and great glory.

The New Testament knows nothing of Christ returning again as an infant in the form of another person. The Second Coming will be a cataclysmic worldwide event viewed by the entire human race. Baha'u'llah falls extremely short of the biblical presentation of Christ's Second Coming. In fact, Jesus has warned us of individuals like Baha'u'llah. He says:

For many will come in my name, claiming, "I am the Christ," and will deceive many. . . At that time if anyone says to you, "Look, here is the Christ!" or, "There he is!" do not believe it. (Matt. 24:5, 23)

Jesus Christ Rose Bodily from the Grave

According to 'Abdu'l-Baha', Christ's Resurrection was merely symbolic. It was the teachings and perfections of Jesus which compelled the Apostles to proclaim the Gospel to all nations. There was no physical resurrection.[44]

In fact, 'Abdu'l-Baha' dispenses with the whole concept of the miraculous (prior to looking at any fact). He writes:

Wherever in the Holy Books they speak of raising the dead, the meaning is that the dead were blessed by eternal life; where it is said that the blind received sight, the signification is that he obtained the true perception; where it is said that a deaf man received hearing, the meaning is that he acquired spiritual and heavenly hearing. This ascertained from the text of the Gospel where Christ said: "These are like those of whom Isaiah said, They have eyes and see not, they have ears and hear not."[45]

Once again the Baha'i apologist commits the same fallacy as before. Without examining the text of the New Testament, he presupposes at the outset that any reference to the miraculous is symbolic. However, in this case, the presupposition is allegedly justified by a passage which the Baha'is arbitrarily deem to be nonsymbolic (the above quote from Christ of Isaiah) in Matt. 13:14. But he is not talking about a symbolic interpretation of His miraculous healings and resurrection, as 'Abdu'l-Baha' assumes. He is talking about feeding the four thousand and the five thousand. The text reads:

Aware of their discussion, Jesus asked them: "Why are you talking about having no bread? Do you still not see or understand? Are your hearts hardened? Do you have eyes but fail to see, and ears but fail to hear? And don't you remember? When I broke the five loaves for the five thousand, how many basketfuls of pieces did you pick up?" "Twelve," they replied. "And when I broke the seven loaves for the four thousand, how many basketfuls of pieces did you pick up?" They answered, "Seven." He said to them, "Do you still not understand?" (Mark 8:17–21)

In another passage where Christ gives a more direct quote of Isaiah, He is talking about the spiritual blindness of those who disbelieve, and their inability to understand His message apart from the use of parables. His statement in no way justifies the Baha'i presupposition. The text reads:

This is why I speak to them in parables: Though seeing, they do not see; though hearing, they do not hear or understand. In them is fulfilled the prophecy of Isaiah: "You will be ever hearing but never understanding; you will be ever seeing but never perceiving." (Matt. 13:13–14)

When the text of the New Testament is examined, it becomes clear to the reader that the text teaches the physical resurrection of Jesus. John 2:19–21 reads:

Jesus answered them, "Destroy this temple, and I will raise it again in three days." The Jews replied, "It has taken forty-six years to build this temple, and you are going to raise it in three days?" But the temple he had spoken of was his body.

The Greek word for *body* in this passage is *soma (σῶμα)*. According to Greek scholar Joseph Thayer, the word *soma* refers to the physical body in this context.[46] After the resurrection, Jesus told Thomas to put his fingers into a physical body (John 20:27–29), not a symbolic illusion. When the disciples mistook Christ as a spirit, He responded by saying:

> Look at my hands and my feet. It is I myself! Touch me and see; a ghost does not have flesh and bones, as you see I have. (Luke 24:39)

Since the Baha'is cannot justify their presupposition of Biblical interpretation, and since the text of the New Testament clearly teaches the bodily Resurrection of Jesus Christ from the dead, we must stand with the Apostle Paul, who wrote:

> And if Christ has not been raised, our preaching is useless and so is your faith. (1 Cor. 15:14)

Jesus Christ Is the Only Savior for All Eternity

The fact that the New Testament teaches that Jesus Christ is the only way to heaven is not denied by the Baha'i religion. The Baha'is deny that Jesus is the only Savior for *all eternity*. They believe He was only the Savior, or manifestation of God, for His dispensation. This dispensation ended with Muhammed and the religion of Islam. However, the question we now face is: Does the New Testament teach that Jesus Christ is *not* the Savior for all eternity? In John 14:6, Jesus had this to say:

> Jesus answered, "I am the way and the truth and the life. No one comes to the Father except through me."

Though the text does not say that He is the only way for all eternity, nevertheless, we cannot assume that Christ meant that his statement was limited to a particular era, unless the text permits it. It does not.

In Acts 4:12, the Apostle Peter said of his Master:

> Salvation is found in no one else, for there is no other name under heaven given to men by which we must be saved.

Once again, the Baha'is must presuppose that Peter meant that Jesus was the only way to God for that era, in order to prove their point. Since the text does not render such an interpretation, there is no ground for the presupposition. In Matt. 28:19–20, Jesus tells His disciples that His teachings are to be taught until the end of the world. The text reads:

> Therefore go and make disciples of all nations, baptizing them in the name of the Father and of the Son and of the Holy Spirit, and teaching them to obey everything I have commanded you. And surely I will be with you always, to the very end of the age.

Since we have already demonstrated that Baha'u'llah is not Christ returned, because of his failure to fulfill particular biblical criteria (i.e., being seen by all eyes, coming down in the clouds, etc.), the end of the age has not yet occurred. Since Christ's teachings include the doctrine of Him being the only way to heaven (John 14:6), and we are commanded to preach *all* His teachings until the end of the age (Christ's return), therefore, Jesus is still the only way by which men can be saved.

Some Baha'is have pointed out that the word *age* in Matthew 28:20 is referring *not* to the end of the world, but to the end of Christ's dispensation (ending with Muhammed's arrival).[47] The problem with this argument, is that it attacks a "straw man." For example, Matt. 24:3 reads:

> As Jesus was sitting on the Mount of Olives, the disciples came to him privately. "Tell us," they said, "when will this happen, and what will be the sign of your coming and of the end of the age?"

The Greek word for *age* in this passage is the same one Christ used in Matt. 28:20, *aionos (αἰῶνος).*[48] Therefore we can be reasonably certain that Jesus was talking about the same "end of the age" in both passages. One need only turn to Matt. 24 and read Christ's description of the end of the age, and one will immediately notice that the end of the age is the same as Christ's Second Coming, which we have already demonstrated that Baha'u'llah did not fulfill. Whether one calls it the "end of the world," "end of the age," or "end of the dispensation" makes no difference. Since Christ has not returned, we have not reached the end of whatever-you'd-like-to-call-it.

CONCLUSION

The attributes of God, as revealed by God's alleged manifestations are contradictory beyond reconciliation. The Baha'i doctrine of revelation is self-defeating, and the criteria for manifestations do not fit all those considered to be manifestations. The Baha'i objections to the traditional doctrines of the Incarnation, the Resurrection, the Second Coming, and the uniqueness of Jesus Christ, are all based on very weak arguments. Thus, based on our study of Baha'i doctrine, it is neither logically nor theologically compelling enough to command our belief.

Chapter 4

THE BAHA'I USE OF THE BIBLE

'Abdu'l-Baha' has correctly observed that "there are some people who, even if all the proofs in the world be adduced before them, still will not judge justly."[1] It is our contention concerning the Baha'i proofs, that we examine the evidence and judge it on its own merits in a fair and impartial manner.

The following chapter will include seven Biblical passages often employed by Baha'i apologists, the Baha'i explanation of each passage, and a Christian critique of each Baha'i explanation. We will conclude this chapter with the examination of a little-known Baha'i false prophecy.

DANIEL 8:13–17

Then I heard a holy one speaking, and another holy one said to him, "How long will it take for the vision to be fulfilled—the vision concerning the daily sacrifice, the rebellion that causes desolation, and the surrender of the sanctuary and of the host that will be trampled underfoot?" He said to me, "It will take 2,300 evenings and mornings; then the sanctuary will be reconstructed." While I, Daniel, was watching the vision and trying to understand it, there before me stood one who looked like a man. And I heard a man's voice from the Ulai calling, "Gabriel, tell this man the meaning of the vision." As he came near the place where I was standing, I was terrified and fell prostrate. "Son of man," he said to me, "understand that the vision concerns the time of the end."

Baha'i Explanation

Concerning this passage, 'Abdu'l-Baha' writes:

Briefly the purport of this passage is that he appoints two thousand three-hundred years, for in the text of the Bible each day is a year. Then from the date of the issuing of the edict of Artaxerxes to rebuild Jerusalem until the day of the birth of Christ there are 456 years, and from the birth of Christ until the day of the manifestation of the Bab there are 1844 years. When you add 456 to the remainder it makes 2,300 years. That is to say, the fulfillment of the vision of Daniel took place in the year 1844 A.D., and this is the year of the Bab's manifestation according to the actual text of the Book of Daniel. Consider how clearly he determines the year of the manifestations and there could be no clearer prophecy for a manifestation than this.[2]

To buttress this position, 'Abdu'l-Baha' cites the fact that Daniel 9 accurately prophesied Christ's first coming. He points out that "seventy 'sevens' are decreed for your people and your holy city. . ." (Dan. 9:24). According to 'Abdu'l-Baha', if one accepts the fact that the Jews reckoned these seventy weeks as 490 years (a "seven" equaling a seven-year period), and assumes that this 490 year period began from Artaxerxes' edict to rebuild the temple in 457 B.C., this conclusion is rendered:

> The third edict of Artaxerxes was issued four hundred and fifty-seven years before the birth of Christ, and Christ when he was martyred was thirty-three years of age. When you add thirty-three to four hundred and fifty-seven, the result is four hundred and ninety, which is the time announced by Daniel for the manifestation of Christ.[3]

Reckoning from the 457 B.C. edict of Artaxerxes, 'Abdu'l-Baha' takes the 2,300 "years" of Dan. 8:13–17 and arrives at A.D. 1844. Thus, he "proves" that the Babi-Baha'i religion is prophesied in the Bible. By establishing the prophetic fulfillment of Christ's first coming, 'Abdu'l-Baha' has left the Christian with what appears to be a difficult dilemma: If one accepts the prophecy of Christ in Daniel 9, then one is forced, reasons 'Abdu'l-Baha', to accept the prophecy in Daniel 8 which allegedly predicts the coming of the Bab. On the other hand, if the Christian rejects both Daniel prophecies, he then is forced into doubting the authority of the Scriptures, the source of his religious knowledge.

A Christian Response

'Abdu'l-Baha's interpretation of this passage must be rejected for two reasons: (A) When interpreting another time prophecy in the same chapter, 'Abdu'l-Baha's rule of interpretation (hermeneutic) produced a false prophecy; and (B) There's no reason to suppose that 2,300 evenings and mornings refer to years.

Objection (A) will not be dealt with here, but will be presented in "Baha'i Watergate," the final section of this chapter. However, concerning objection (B), several points should be brought out.

To begin with, 'Abdu'l-Baha' makes the assumption that because the seventy "sevens" of Dan. 9 are almost universally interpreted to mean 490 years, therefore, the 2,300 evenings and mornings must also be interpreted as years. This reasoning is incorrect because it does not take into account that a seven (a week) can be biblically justified to mean a seven-year period, but an evening and a morning cannot be justified to mean a one year period. Writes Robert D. Culver, Th.D.:

> The Hebrew word for *week (shabu'im)*, "sevens," means "sevens" of years. This interpretation was the common one in antiquity. Daniel had been thinking of a multiple of "sevens" of years (9:12; cf. Jer 25:11,12). He knew that multiple (seventy years) to be an epoch of judgment—for 490 years of violated sabbaths (490 ÷ 7 = 70. see II Chr 36:21). Furthermore, there was a

common "seven" of years employed in civil and religious reckoning (Lev 25, esp. v. 8) quite as aptly called a "week" as the seven of days. Not only so, but when weeks of days are intended (Dan 10:2,3), the Hebrew word for "days" *(yamin)*, is added to "weeks" *(shabu'im)*. This apparently indicates a break from the use of chapter 9. More importantly, if any literal meaning is to be attached to the weeks, no period less than weeks of years meets the contextual demands. *Upon thy holy people and upon thy holy city.* The people Jews; the city is Jerusalem.[4]

There is no similar evidence, within the biblical text, to indicate that "an evening and a morning" can be interpreted to mean a year. However, concerning the actual meaning of the 2,300 evenings and mornings, Charles Lee Feinberg, dean emeritus of Talbot Theological Seminary, had this to say:

. . .the desolation was to last "for 2,300 evenings and mornings" and was to end with the cleansing of the Temple. Antiochus began his oppression of the Jews in 171 B.C.; and it was 2,300 days later, in December of 165 B.C., that it ended with the cleansing of the Temple by Judas Maccabaeus.

Failure to understand the exact nature of this prophecy has led many to blunder into even more grave errors that touch at the very heart of our faith. It was from the misinterpretation of this verse that the whole system of Seventh Day Adventism arose. It must be stressed that those 2,300 days have already run their course in the history of the Jews; nothing is said here about a future people or a future period of time.

As we said, in 165 B.C. Judas Maccabaeus fulfilled this prophecy by cleansing the defiled sanctuary. He designated a new priesthood to minister in the Temple, and he pulled down the defiling heathen altar that had been erected there. He carried out all the defiled stones to an unclean place and built a new altar in place of the old one Antiochus had defiled. He repaired the courts; replaced the altar of incense, the table of the bread of the Presence, and the golden lampstands; and he rededicated them all to the sole service of God. This rededication occurred on the twenty fifth day of Chislev and was celebrated for eight days. It was known as the Feast of Lights, or the Feast of Dedication, and is still celebrated anually by the Jews at Chanukah, which means "dedication" (cf. John 10:22).[5]

Another reason to reject the Baha'i interpretation of this passage is the fact that there is no reason to suppose that the 2,300 "evenings and mornings," if they were to mean "years," should be counted from Artaxerxes' decree to rebuild Jerusalem. And even if we were to grant to the Baha'is the legitimacy of counting 2,300 years from Artaxerxes' decree, they would still be incorrect in their calculations.

'Abdu'l-Baha' states that Artaxerxes' decree was given in 457 B.C. This is not accurate. According to his most recent research, Josh McDowell has fixed the date of Artaxerxes' decree to rebuild Jerusalem at 444 B.C.[6] In light of the fact that a Jewish prophetic year equals 360 days (not 365 days), counting from 444 B.C., we arrive at approximately A.D. 1823.[7] Thus, 'Abdu'l-Baha's interpretation is clearly incorrect.

One may wonder if McDowell's date of Artaxerxes's decree damages the validity of the prophecy of Christ's coming in Dan. 9. On the contrary, it puts it on a firmer foundation. Dan. 9:25 states that from "the issuing of the decree to restore and rebuild Jerusalem until the Annointed One (Messiah), the ruler, comes, there will be seven 'sevens,' and sixty-two 'sevens.' " 'Abdu'l-Baha' incorrectly stated that there would be seventy "sevens" from the decree of Artaxerxes until the announcement of Christ.[8] According to the text, there are seventy "sevens" decreed for the people and the holy city (Dan. 9:24), but sixty-nine "sevens" until the coming of the Messiah (Dan. 9:25). In light of the above evidence, McDowell writes:

> If Daniel is correct, the time from the edict to restore and rebuild Jerusalem (Nisan 1, 444 B.C.) to the coming of the Messiah is 483 years (69×7), each year equaling the Jewish prophetic year of 360 days (173,880).

> The terminal event of the 69 weeks is the presentation of Christ Himself to Israel as the Messiah as predicted in Zechariah 9:9. H. Hoehner, who has thoroughly researched this prophecy in Daniel, and the corresponding dates, calculates the date of this event: "Multiplying the sixty-nine weeks by seven years for each week by 360 days gives a total of 173,880. The difference between 444 B.C. and A.D. 33 then is 476 solar years. By multiplying 476 by 365.24219879 or by 365 days, 5 hours, 48 minutes, 45.975 seconds [365.25 days in a year] . . . , one comes to 173,855 days. This leaves only 25 days to be accounted for between 444 B.C. and A.D. 33. By adding 25 days to March 5 (of 444 B.C.), one comes to March 30 (or A.D. 33) which was Nisan 10 in A.D. 33. This is the triumphal entry of Jesus into Jerusalem."[9]

From the above evidence, it can be concluded that the Baha'i apologist has no basis in appealing to Daniel 8 as a prophetic foundation for his religion.

ISAIAH 11:1–10

> A shoot will come up from the stump of Jesse; from his roots a Branch will bear fruit. The Spirit of the Lord will rest on him—the Spirit of wisdom and of understanding, the Spirit of counsel and of power, the Spirit of knowledge and of the fear of the Lord. He will not judge by what he sees with his eyes, or decide by what he hears with his ears; but with righteousness he will judge the needy, with justice he will give decisions for the poor of the earth. He will strike the earth with the rod of his mouth; with the breath of his lips he will slay the wicked. Righteousness will be his belt and faithfulness the sash around his waist. The wolf will live with the lamb, the leopard will lie down with the goat, the calf and the lion and the yearling together; and a little child will lead them. The cow will feed with the bear, their young will lie down together, and the lion will eat straw with the ox. The infant will play near the hole of the cobra, and the young child put his hand into the viper's nest. They will neither harm nor destroy all my holy mountain, for the earth will be full of the knowledge of the Lord as the waters cover the sea. In that day the Root of Jesse will stand as a banner for the peoples; the nations will rally to him, and his place of rest will be glorious.

Baha'i Explanation

'Abdu'l-Baha' interprets this passage in the following manner:

> The rod out of the stem of Jesse might be correctly applied to Jesus Christ, for Joseph was of the descendents of Jesse the father of David. . .

> . . . the events which he indicated as coming to pass in the days of the rod, if interpreted symbolically, were in part fulfilled in the day of Christ, but not all; and if not interpreted, then decidedly none of these signs happened. For example, the leopard and the lamb, the lion and the calf, the child and the asp, are metaphors and symbols of various nations, peoples, antagonistic sects, and hostile races, who are so opposite and inimical as the wolf and the lamb. We say that by the breath of the spirit of Christ they found concord and . . . were vivified, and they associated together. [10]

Concerning Isaiah's prophecy that "they will neither harm nor destroy on all my holy mountain. . ." (v. 9), 'Abdu'l-Baha' had this to say:

> These conditions did not prevail in the time of the manifestation of Christ; for until today various and antagonistic nations exist in the world, very few acknowledge the God of Israel, and the greater number are without the knowledge of God. In the same way, universal peace did not come into existence in the time of Christ; that is to say, between the antagonistic and hostile nations there was neither peace nor concord, disputes and disagreements did not cease. . .

> But these verses apply word for word to Baha'u'llah: likewise in this marvelous cycle the earth will be transformed, and the world of humanity arrayed in tranquility and beauty. Disputes, quarrels, and murders will be replaced by peace, truth and concord; among the nations, peoples, races, and countries, love and amity will appear. Co-operation and unity will be established, and finally war will be surpressed. [11]

This prophecy, according to 'Abdu'l-Baha', must be fulfilled in the person of Baha'u'llah. The programs Baha'u'llah has set up for world peace and unity verifies this conviction.

> Now see: these events did not take place in the Christian cycle, for the nations did not come under One standard which is the Divine Branch. [12]

A Christian Response

'Abdu'l-Baha's interpretation of Isaiah 11:1–10 fails to take into account two points: (1) The context of the passage; and (2) The dual nature of Christ's mission.

'Abdu'l-Baha' ignores context when he interprets the first part of the passage as referring to Jesus (the stump of Jesse), and the second part of the passage as referring to Baha'u'llah. Isaiah clearly begins the passage with reference to the individual he is writing about, the stump of Jesse (11:1). From that point onward Isaiah continually refers to all the things that this descendent of Jesse will do. Isaiah, again in v.10, writes of whom he is speaking: "In that day the Root of Jesse. . ." It is clear that the descendant of Jesse is the primary subject of the passage. Jesus was a descendant of Jesse (Matt. 1:16); Baha'u'llah was not. Therefore, by virtue of Isaiah's criterion, Baha'u'llah was unable to fulfill this prophecy.

'Abdu'l-Baha' also points out that Jesus did not bring the peace that was prophesied by Isaiah. He argues that Baha'u'llah did propose a plan for world peace, and therefore, has fulfilled this prophecy. We believe this argument lacks real substance. For any reasonable person knows that proposing a plan for peace and actually carrying it out are two entirely different things. Though the possibility exists that at some future unforseen date the Baha'i faith may achieve world peace by employing Baha'u'llah's method, it has yet to do so. Therefore, Baha'u'llah did not fulfill this prophecy.

Since Jesus is the root of Jesse, why is there not the worldwide tranquility as outlined in Isaiah? Why hasn't the lion laid down with the lamb? The dual nature of Christ's mission explains this apparent inconsistency. Jesus admitted that His first coming was not intended to bring peace. Quoting Jesus, Matthew writes:

> Do not suppose that I have come to bring peace to the earth. I did not come to bring peace, but a sword. For I have come to turn a man against his father, a daughter against her mother, a daughter-in-law against her mother-in-law— a man's enemies will be the members of his own household. (10:34–36)

On the other hand, Jesus did say that those who would follow Him would have an inward peace that the world could not give (John 14:2). It is apparent that Jesus' message brings discord between believers and unbelievers (Matt. 10:34–36), but gives an inward peace to those who put their trust in Christ (John 14:2).

Though Jesus did not promise world peace at His first coming, He did promise to return (Matt. 24). Upon His return He will set up a kingdom of world unity and peace (Rev. 21), and He will judge both the living and the dead (Rev. 20:11–15 cf. Matt. 25:31–46). We have no reason to suppose that Christ's Second Coming refers to anyone else but Jesus of Nazareth (see Chapter 3). In light of the fact that Jesus did verify His claims to Deity by rising from the dead (see Chapter 5), we have good reason to suppose that He was telling the truth about His Second Coming. This differs from Baha'u'llah's utopian dreams, which are merely imaginary proposals not grounded in any verifiable fact or event.

JOHN 16:12–13

> I have much more to say to you, more than you can now bear. But when he, the Spirit of truth, comes, he will guide you into all truth. He will speak only what he hears, and he will tell you what is yet to come.

Baha'i Explanation

According to Cheney, the "Baha'is believe that Baha'u'llah is that Spirit of Truth foretold by Jesus. . ."[13]

Jesus the Christ . . . foresaw a day of greater maturity when the world would be able to receive a fuller measure of that same truth, and He promised that, when the day dawned, another would come who would be like Himself, who would come in the glory of the Father, and who would bring that further truth which the world would then be able to receive.[14]

A Christian Response

The problem with Cheney's interpretaion is that it does not take into account the context of the passage. In the same discourse Jesus calls this Spirit of Truth *the Counselor* (John 15:26). Earlier in the discourse He calls this Counselor the *Holy Spirit*:

All this I have spoken while still with you. But the Counselor, the Holy Spirit, whom the Father will send in my name, will teach you all things and will remind you of everything I have said to you. (John 14:25–26)

Jesus gave specific instructions concerning the arrival of this Spirit of Truth:

Do not leave Jerusalem, but wait for the gift my Father promised, which you have heard me speak about. For John baptized with water, but in a few days you will be baptized with the Holy Spirit. (Acts 1:4–5)

This Counselor (Holy Spirit and Spirit of Truth) was received by Christ's disciples on the day of Pentecost. Writes Luke:

When the day of Pentecost came, they were all together in one place. Suddenly a sound like the blowing of a violent wind came from heaven and filled the whole house where they were sitting. They saw what seemed to be tongues of fire that separated and came to rest on each of them. All of them were filled with the Holy Spirit and began to speak in other tongues as the Spirit enabled them. (Acts 2:1–2)

Therefore, the biblical record, rather than supporting the Baha'i claim, categorically denies it.

ISAIAH 35:1–2

The desert and the parched land will be glad; the wilderness will rejoice and blossom. Like the crocus, it will burst into bloom; it will rejoice greatly and shout for joy. The glory of Lebanon will be given to it, the splendor of Carmel and Sharon; they will see the glory of the Lord, the splendor of our God.

Baha'i Explanation

According to Cheney, Baha'u'llah was banished to a solitary desert place (the prison of 'Akka' in Palestine), and taught upon Mount Carmel and in the Valley of Sharon. Therefore, these places "quite literally saw the Glory of the Lord through His Manifestation, just as Isaiah had promised." "Baha'u'llah," writes Cheney, "translated into English means the Glory of

God, the title frequently given by the Bible to the Manifestation of the latter days."[15]

A Christian Response

It is unfortunate for the Baha'i position that Ms. Cheney commits the fallacy of begging the question. According to the Baha'i apologist, the fact that Baha'u'llah taught upon Mt. Carmel and in the Valley of Sharon proves that he fulfills this prophecy. Since many have taught upon Mt. Carmel and in the Valley of Sharon, to cite this prophecy as proof of Baha'u'llah's divine mission is absurd. However, Cheney qualifies her claim by stating that these places (Carmel and Sharon), according to the prophecy, will see "the glory of the Lord," and that in Baha'u'llah "these places literally saw the Glory of the Lord through His Manifestation."[16]

The fact that Baha'u'llah's *title* means "the glory of God," does not prove that he is "the glory of God" (in a positional sense). First it must be proven that Baha'u'llah *is* the "glory of God," apart from his bestowing the title upon himself. According to Cheney, we know that Baha'u'llah is the fulfillment of Isaiah's prophecy because he is "the glory of God." On the other hand, we know that he is "the glory of God," because he is the fulfillment of Isaiah's prophecy. The argument begs the question, and is, therefore false.

The Baha'i usage of the Isaiah passage also should be rejected in light of its context. Neither chapter 35 nor the chapter preceding it either imply or affirm the coming of a Persian prophet (such as Baha'u'llah) who will bring world peace and unity. The burden of proof rests on the Baha'i apologist to demonstrate why this passage can be interpreted in such a fashion, apart from the use of question-begging arguments.

ISAIAH 9:1, 6, 7

The people walking in darkness have seen a great light; on those living in the land of the shadow of death a light has dawned.

For to us a child is born, to us a son is given, and the government will be on his shoulders. And he will be called Wonderful Counselor, Mighty God, Everlasting Father, Prince of Peace. Of the increase of his government and peace there will be no end. He will reign on David's throne and over his kingdom, establishing and upholding it with justice and righteousness from that time on and forever. The zeal of the Lord Almighty will accomplish this.

Baha'i Explanation

According to Cheney, Jesus could not fulfill this prophecy because "He had nothing to say concerning 'government' (v. 7) except 'Render unto Caesar the things that are Caesar's and unto God the things that are God's.' "[17] Cheney states that this is one of the reasons why the Jews rejected Christ. They misunderstood this prophecy and "thought that it must be fulfilled in the day of Christ." They did not realize that Isaiah was referring to the "time of the end, when the thousand years of peace promised by Isaiah (11:6–9 and 65:21–25), and later in the Christian dispensation by John the Divine (Rev. 20:1–3), were to be fulfilled."[18]

According to Cheney, there are two other reasons why Jesus did not fulfill this prophecy: (A) Jesus never claimed to be the Prince of Peace (v. 6b); and (B) Jesus was never known as the "Father" (v.6b). In contrast, Cheney presents several reasons why Baha'is teach that Baha'u'llah is the fulfillment of these prophecies. She writes:

> The light of Baha'u'llah shone forth from Iran, the darkest, most bigoted, ignorant, and misgoverned part of the world of His day. In some one hundred books, which He wrote during forty years of imprisonment, Baha'u'llah out-lined a complete plan of government for the day of world peace, many phases of which are becoming generally accepted by outstanding thinkers of this day, such as a world federation of all nations, an international tribunal, and an international police force to maintain peace. Baha'u'llah is known as the Manifestation of the Father in the sense of being One who unites and brings together into one common family under God all religions, all races, and all nations.[19]

A Christian Response

Cheney states that Isaiah was referring to the "time of the end, when the thousand years of peace promised by Isaiah . . . and later in the Christian dispensation by John the Divine . . . were to be fulfilled."[20] We have already demonstrated that Christ's Second Coming, which will bring about the es-tablishment of His kingdom and world peace (Rev. 21–22), refers only to the personal return of Jesus of Nazareth at the "time of the end" (Chapter 3). In fact, John the Divine, quoted by Cheney as an authoritative source concerning the "time of the end,"[21] knows nothing of the return of anyone else but Jesus of Nazareth. Writes John: "He who testifies to these things says, 'Yes, I am coming soon.' Amen. Come, Lord Jesus" (Rev. 22:20). Thus, the "time of the end" will usher in only the return of Jesus of Nazareth.

Cheney writes that Christ did not call Himself the "Prince of Peace," nor was He known as the "Father." Concerning the title of *Prince of Peace*, Gleason Archer, Professor of Old Testament and Semitics at Trinity Evan-gelical Divinity School, had this to say:

> As Prince of Peace, he will bestow what *shalom*, "peace," implies in its fullest meaning: health to the sin-sick soul; a sound and healthy relation between sinners and God, as well as between sinners and fellow sinners; and a sound condition of universal righteousness and prosperity prevailing over the earth.[22]

This, of course, is fulfilled in the person of Jesus, who in His first coming paid the price necessary for the salvation of men's souls. Thus, establishing peace between God and man (Rom. 5:9–10). In His Second Coming, Christ will establish a kingdom that will bear the fruit of world peace (Rev. 21–22).

In reference to the problem of Christ not being known as the *Everlasting Father*, Archer writes:

"Isaiah 9:6 says of the common savior, 'His name shall be called Wonderful Counselor, Mighty God, *Everlasting Father*, Prince of Peace.' At least this is the way it is usually translated. But the basis for doing so is rather dubious, since the Hebrew . . . literally means 'Father of Eternity' . . . In view of the above, it seems reasonable to understand . . . 'Father of Eternity' in the sense of 'Author of Eternity' . . ."[23]

The position of "Father of Eternity," or "Author of Eternity" is attributed to Jesus in John 1:3. It reads: "Through him all things were made; without him nothing was made that has been made."

It is also important to note that Isaiah states that this "Prince of Peace" will reign "on David's throne and over his kingdom. . ." (9:7). According to the Scriptures, David's throne can only be occupied by someone who is a descendant of David (2 Sam. 7:5–16). Baha'u'llah is not a descendant of David, and therefore, cannot rightfully claim to fulfill Isaiah's prophecy. On the other hand, both Matthew (1:1, 6, 17) and Luke (3:23–31) state that Jesus is a descendent of David. In fact, John quotes Jesus as saying:

I, Jesus, have sent my angel to give you this testimony for the churches. I am the Root and the Offspring of David, and the bright Morning Star. (Rev. 22:16)

Though Baha'u'llah has outlined a plan for world peace and claimed to be a manifestation of the Father, it cannot be concluded, on that basis, that he is indeed the Everlasting Father and the Prince of Peace spoken of by Isaiah. It is one thing to claim something is true, it is quite another to verify it. As we have pointed out, Christ verified His claims by physical resurrection (see Chapter 5). Therefore, we have excellent reason to believe that what Christ has said about His first and second comings is true.

BAHA'I WATERGATE:
A FALSE PROPHECY AND ITS COVER-UP

In his 1923 edition of *Baha'u'llah and the New Era*, J.E. Esslemont wrote:

Both Baha'u'llah and 'Abdu'l-Baha' predict in most confident terms the speedy triumph of spirituality over materiality and the consequent establishment of the Most Great Peace.[24]

Referring to 'Abdu'l-Baha', Esslemont continues:

He declares that this consummation is near at hand and will come about during the present century. In an address to Theosophists in February 1913, he said: "This Century is the Century of the Sun of Trust. This Century is the Century of the establishment of the Kingdom of God upon the earth."— *Star of the West*, vol. ix p. 7. In the last two verses of the Book of Daniel occur the cryptic words:—"Blessed is he that waiteth and cometh to the thousand, three hundred and thirty-five days. But go thy way till the end can be: for thou shalt rest, and stand in thy lot at the end of the days." Many have been the attempts of learned students to solve the problem of the significance of these words. In a table-talk at which the writer was present,

'Abdu'l-Baha' said:—"These 1,335 days mean 1,335 solar years from Hijrat (Flight of Muhammad from Mecca to Medina, marking the beginning of the Muhammaden era.) As the Hijrat occurred in 622 A.D. the date referred to is, therefore, 1957 (i.e. 622 + 1,335) A.D. Asked: "What shall we see at the end of the 1,335 days?" he replied: "Universal Peace will be firmly established, a Universal language promoted. Misunderstandings will pass away. The Baha'i Cause will be promulgated in all parts and the oneness of mankind established!"[25]

In the 1970 edition of this book (the 3rd revision after the author's death), 'Abdu'l-Baha's false prophecy is missing, and Esslemont's testimony of 'Abdu'l-Baha's "table-talk" has been strangely altered. The newest edition reads (altered and added sections are italized—author's emphasis):

In the last two verses of the Book of Daniel occur the cryptic words:—"Blessed is he that waiteth and cometh to the thousand, three hundred and thirty-five days. But go thy way till the end be: for thou shalt rest, and stand in thy lot at the end of the days." Many have been the attempts of learned students to solve this problem of the significance of these words. In a table-talk at which the writer was present, 'Abdu'l-Baha' *reckoned the fulfillment of Daniel's prophecy from the date of the beginning of the Muhammaden Era. 'Abdu'l-Baha's Tablets make it clear that this prophecy refers to the one hundreth anniversary of the Declaration of Baha'u'llah in Baghdad, or the year 1963:—* "Now concerning the verse in Daniel, the interpretation where of thou didst ask, 'Blessed is he who cometh unto the thousand, three hundred and thirty-five days.' These days must be reckoned as solar and not lunar years. For according to this calculation a century will have elapsed from the dawn of the Sun of the Truth, then will the teachings of God be firmly established upon the earth, and the divine light shall flood the world from East even unto West. Then on this day will the faithful rejoice!"[26]

The Baha'i claim that 'Abdu'l-Baha's statement from his Tablets makes it clear that Daniel's prophecy refers to the one hundreth anniversary of Baha'u'llah's Declaration in Baghdad (1963) is *weak*. One need only to read the above statement from the Tablets (the italicized portion) to see that it in no way conflicts with 'Abdu'l-Baha's claim that Universal Peace will be established in 1957 (conspicuously absent from the 1970 edition). In fact, you really have to read the hundreth anniversary into the text in order to find it. Apparently 'Abdu'l-Baha' had a change of mind after his death?

Those who altered Esslemont's original work probably thought that nobody would recognize the absence of the false prophecy in the 1970 edition, and therefore chose to reinterpret 'Abdu'l-Baha's statement in his Tablets so that it would appear that he was *not* referring to a specific date in the 20th Century (1957) in which Universal Peace would be established. This is clearly a case of censorship, and conflicts with the Baha'i principle of "a free investigation of truth." It is interesting that the Baha'i Publishing Committee, which censored the embarrassing false prophecy, altered the eyewitness testimony of a man after his death (remember, Esslemont was *there* at 'Abdu'l-Baha's table-talk). Considering the magnitude of the passage, such an action is absolutely unethical. Since world peace did not occur in 1957,

'Abdu'l-Baha' is a false prophet. Deut. 18:21–22 reads:

> You may say to yourselves, "How can we know when a message has not been spoken by the Lord?" If what a prophet proclaims in the name of the Lord does not take place or come true, that is a message the Lord has not spoken. That prophet has spoken presumptuously. Do not be afraid of him.

CONCLUSION

From the standpoint of doctrinal defense, the Baha'i use of the Bible is a miserable failure. However, from the standpoint of revealing the ethical character and depth of biblical scholarship on the part of the Baha'is, it serves a most useful purpose.

For instance, we have seen through their writings, that the chief representatives of Baha'i scholarship show an absolute ignorance of properly interpreting any given biblical text. They ignore context, language, intent, and historical setting. They seek only to twist biblical passages so as to fit their presupposed doctrines which, in their opinion, justify these presupposed doctrines. This seems to be the continuing fallacy lurking behind almost every Baha'i apologetic use of the Bible: Baha'i apologists (defenders) reason in a circle.

Concerning ethical character, upon which the Baha'is put a premium, the censorship of J. E. Esslemont's book, after his death, is indeed a black mark upon all Baha'ism. Changing an eyewitness testimony (of 'Abdu'l-Baha's false prophecy) after the death of the eyewitness is blatantly unethical.

Chapter 5

ON THE TRUTH OF CHRISTIANITY

JUDGING RELIGIOUS TRUTH CLAIMS

Abu Qurra and Religious Truth

Theodore Abu Qurra, a ninth century Syrian theologian and bishop of Harran in Mesopotamia, wrote a parable which, we believe, accurately describes the situation we are faced with in a world containing a multitude of religious options. John Warwick Montgomery paraphrases it in the following quote:

> A great king (God) had a son (mankind) who had grown up out of contact with his father. While journeying in a distant province the son fell seriously ill. The doctor accompanying him (reason) was incapable of treating the disease, but the king, learning of his son's plight, sent instructions (the gospel) for the healing of the boy. However, the king's numerous enemies also discovered what had happened, and they likewise sent remedies . . . which were actually poisonous (non-Christian religious and philosophical options). The son's solution to this dilemma was to evaluate the remedies by three tests: first, what each remedy revealed about his father (comparison being made with the likeness to the father possessed by the son himself); second, how accurately each remedy pictured the nature of the disease; and thirdly, how sound the various curative methods appeared to be. . . [1]

We do not agree with Abu Qurra's first test—comparing the likeness of the father possessed by the son with what each remedy allegedly revealed about the father's nature. This carries the possible danger of attributing aspects of the son's own wickedness to his father (God). But we believe there is some validity in the remaining two tests.

These two tests—first, the accuracy of picturing the nature of man's illness and, second, the soundness of the alleged cure of his illness—are both universal in scope and are able to meet man at the point of his ultimate personal need. In addition, it can be reasonably assumed (to satisfy the third test of Abu Qurra's parable) if we discover the illness of mankind and its remedy, then this remedy has indeed been sent from the father (God).

Death: The Universal Enemy

A religion which is true should deal with the ultimate malady of the human race. Our common malady is known as death. Death is the inevitable, final, complete, devastating, and dreadful fate of every single human being. The late Edward John Carnell describes the situation most accurately:

> The incongruity between man's desire for life and the reality of physical death is the most maddening problem of all. Although he sees the handwriting on the wall, man yet refuses to think that death is his final destiny, that he will perish as the fish and the fowl, and that his place will be remembered no more. Man wills to live forever; the urge is written deep in his nature.[2]

Existential philosophers (those who teach that one should exercise free will in a purposeless universe) have written much about this absurdity. Albert Camus, the French existentialist, has said:

> Likewise and during every day of an unillustrious life, time carries us. But a moment always comes when we have to carry it. We live in the future: "tomorrow," "later on," "when you have made your way," "you will understand when you are old enough." Such irrelevancies are wonderful, for, after all, it's a matter of dying. Yet a day comes when a man notices or says that he is thirty. Thus he asserts his youth. But simultaneously he situates himself in relation to time. He takes his place in it. He admits that he stands at a certain point on a curve that he acknowledges having to travel to its end. He belongs to time, and by the horror that seizes him, he recognizes his worst enemy. Tomorrow, he was longing for tomorrow, whereas everything in him ought to reject it. That revolt of the flesh is the absurd.[3]

Death is man's most obvious enemy. Therefore, is it not reasonable to assume that if the world's religions, which offer the human race countless abstract utopias in the afterlife, cannot deal with man's ultimate dilemma in this mortal realm, they are indeed unworthy to be considered alternatives to the awful truth that "the world itself. . . is but a vast irrational?"[4]

In other words, a religion that is true would be one that defeats death, man's most detestable foe. Of all the religious leaders previously discussed, only one, Jesus of Nazareth, has conquered the Grim Reaper. Though we will all inevitably die, the fact that Jesus defeated death gives us assurance that His pronouncements on the nature of God, His own Deity, salvation, the afterlife, judgment, sin, and righteousness are to be taken most seriously. In fact, the Resurrection of Jesus gives us (believers in Him) the confident hope that we too will be resurrected as He promised.[5] Thus, one day we too will share in the victory over our mortal adversary.

The Fact of the Resurrection

It is important, however, not only to proclaim the resurrection, but also to verify it. Since we claimed the resurrection of Jesus a historical event,[6] it is open to historical falsification as well as verification.

Most of what we know concerning the life, death, and resurrection of Jesus comes from the documents of the New Testament. The writers of the New Testament claim to have been eyewitnesses to the events of Jesus' ministry[7] or, in the case of some New Testament authors, worked as scribes for individuals who were eyewitnesses[8] or had personal access to primary-source documents.[9] If it can be demonstrated that the New Testament documents are historically reliable, beyond any reasonable doubt, we can confidently proclaim that Jesus Christ did indeed destroy man's most hideous inheritance, death.

Probability and Certainty

At this juncture, some may object to investigating historical religious claims, because such claims lack absolute certainty. Most people will not commit themselves to a religion which fails to supply 100% proof. Though this type of demand may appear plausible, and somewhat virtuous to the average observer, it is actually unrealistic and theoretically impossible. Let us explain.

It has been accurately pointed out by most analytic philosophers, that there are only two types of propositions which are considered meaningful in any discussion of truth claims: analytic statements and synthetic statements. An analytic statement is one which does not describe any matter of fact in the world. It deals with statements known as *tautologies*. For instance, mathematical equations are tautologies ($1 + 1$ will always equal 2). For this reason—the fact that they have nothing to do with the real world—analytic propositions are true *by definition*, and are therefore, certainties.

A synthetic statement, on the other hand, is a statement describing a matter of fact in the world of experience and observation. This is the world in which we constantly judge the truth of all matters of fact that confront us. Admittedly, some matters of fact, based on the evidence, are more certain than others (though none of them can reach the level of 100% certainty). For example, the so-called "laws" of nature are only known to be true by observation. Though we do not know with 100% certainty whether these "laws" will function tomorrow as they did yesterday, we still live as if they will. On the other hand, whether Abraham Lincoln was assassinated or not, is not known with 100% certainty. There is a *possibility* that we have all been lied to and that actually Abraham Lincoln slipped on a banana peel while playing pin-the-tail-on-the-donkey. But, the fact of the matter is, the evidence for Lincoln's assassination is so great that it is beyond any reasonable doubt. Sure, it is *possible* that Lincoln's death is not recorded properly in the history books. However, when it comes to investigating facts, we don't live in a world of *possibility*. Rather, we live in a world of *probability* (that which is likely to occur) in which we continually function on the basis of judging the truth or falsity of particular facts (synthetic statements). These facts are judged true or false by the amount of evidence in their favor, not on alternative bizarre possibilities.

This whole discussion of analytic and synthetic propositions is excellently summed up by Hans Hahn, one of the founders of the Vienna Circle:

> We must distinguish two kinds of statements: those which say something about facts and those which merely express the way in which the rules which govern the application of words to facts depend upon each other. Let us call statements of the latter kind *tautologies*: they say nothing about objects and are for that reason certain, universally valid, irrefutable by observation;

whereas statements of the former kind are not certain and are refutable by observation. The logical laws of contradiction and of the excluded middle are tautologies, likewise, e.g., statements "nothing is both red and blue."[10]

To conclude, the historical claims of the Christian faith are just like other facts of history, in the sense that they can be checked out and verified. Though these facts can never rise to the point of 100% certainty, nevertheless, they are no different than other facts. In the case of all matters of fact we must examine the evidence and, based on the quantity and quality of that evidence, make a decision whether or not it is strong enough to command our belief. If, of course, the Christian claims turn out to be the type that can be sufficiently verified, then they are no longer "just like" other facts. In fact, in the particular case of the resurrection, our very souls may hang in the balance.

VERIFICATION OF THE RESURRECTION

In order to verify the fact of Christ's resurrection, we must demonstrate that the New Testament is historically accurate and a reliable piece of historical documentation. "The historical reliability of the Scripture should be tested by the same criteria that all historical documents are tested."[11]

According to C. Sanders, a military historian, in his *Introduction to Research in English Literary History*, there are three principles in determining the historical reliability of any document. These principles are *the bibliographical test, the internal evidence test,* and *the external evidence test.*[12] Each test will be explained and defined, as each is individually applied to the text of the New Testament.

The Bibliographical Test

Josh McDowell explains this test most accurately:

> The Bibliographical test is an examination of the textual transmission by which documents reach us. In other words, since we do not have the original documents, how reliable are the copies we have in regard to the number of manuscripts (MSS) and the time interval between the original and the extant copy.[13]

In order to find out whether or not the New Testament has a bibliographical foundation, we must examine the following elements in the light of the evidence: (a) The amount of existing manuscript copies and their date of composition; (b) The composition date of the original autographs; (c) A comparison of the manuscripts of the New Testament with those of ancient secular history. However, before we proceed, it is important to define what a manuscript is. According to Geisler and Nix, in *A General Introduction to the Bible*:

> A manuscript is a handwritten literary composition in contrast to a printed copy. An original manuscript is the first one produced, usually called an autograph.[14]

The question that presently faces us, however, has to do with the quantity of these New Testament manuscripts. The following is a breakdown of their number and nature.[15]

The John Rylands Fragment: This fragment of a papyrus contains five verses from the book of John. It is dated A.D. 117–138.[16]

The Bodmer Papyri: Dated around A.D. 200, these papyri, which contain most of John's and Luke's Gospels, in addition to the books of Jude, 1 Peter, and 2 Peter, preserve the earliest complete copies of books of the New Testament.

Codex Vaticanus: This manuscript, which contains the whole New Testament, is dated between A.D. 325–350. It also contains the entire Greek Old Testament (LXX) as well.

Codex Sinaiticus: Dating from around A.D. 340, this manuscript contains the whole New Testament and half of the Old Testament.

Codex Ephraemi Rescriptus: This manuscript contains most of the New Testament and part of the Old Testament. It is dated around A.D. 350.

Codex Alexandrinus: This finding, now housed in the British Museum's National Library, is a complete manuscript of the Bible dating from about A.D. 450.

> It should be kept in mind that although the foregoing . . . manuscripts date from the fourth and fifth centuries, they represent in whole or in part an "Alexandrian" (mode Alexandrian, Egypt) type text that dates from A.D. 100–150.[17]

Codex Bazae: This manuscript, dating from A.D. 450 or 550, is written in both Greek and Latin. It contains the four Gospels, the book of Acts, and part of 3 John.

According to New Testament scholar Bruce Metzger, Professor Emeritus of New Testament at Princeton Theological Seminary, there are a total of 4,969 Greek New Testament manuscripts.[18] This, of course, does not include the more than 15,000 existing copies of various versions. These versions include the Syriac and Latin translations of the New Testament which were made around A.D. 150. We have copies of these second century translations dating from the middle of the fourth century to the beginning of the seventh century. These various versions also include Coptic (Egyptian) versions and other early translations dating from the beginning of the third century to the sixth century. When all is said and done there are more than 20,000 known extant manuscripts of the New Testament.[19]

It is important at this juncture that the composition of the original autographs be properly dated:[20]

Matthew A.D. 80–100
Mark A.D. 50–70
Luke A.D. 70–85
John A.D. 90–110
Acts A.D. 70–85
Pauline Epistles A.D. 48–64

Most scholars consider Luke and Acts to be parts of one document. The book of Acts gives a detailed account of the latter portion of the life of the Apostle Paul, but ends abruptly without mentioning that Paul was tried in Rome and martyred under Nero in A.D. 64. Therefore, it would be reasonable to date the Gospel of Luke and the book of Acts prior to A.D. 64.[21]

In fact, William F. Albright, late W.W. Spence Professor of Semitic Languages at Johns Hopkins University, has said:

> In my opinion, every book of the New Testament was written by a baptised Jew between the forties and the eighties of the first century A.D. (very probably sometime between A.D. 50 and 75).[22]

There is very little doubt that the New Testament is a first century historical work. When presenting the *External Evidence Test* below, citations from extra-biblical sources will also validate the New Testament's first century date.

In light of the date of its composition and the abundant quantity of New Testament manuscripts, how does the text fare in comparison to other ancient literature? The following chart should suffice.[23]

Comparison of Ancient Texts

Author	Date Written	Earliest Copy	Time Span	Copies
Caesar	100–44 B.C.	900 A.D.	1000 yrs.	10
Plato (Tetralogies)	427–347 B.C.	900 A.D.	1200 yrs.	7
Tacitus (Annals) and minor works	100 A.D.	1100 A.D.	1000 yrs.	10 (−)
Pliny the Younger (History)	61–113 A.D.	850 A.D.	750 yrs.	7
Thucydides (History)	460–400 B.C.	900 A.D.	1300 yrs.	8
Heroditus (History)	480–425 B.C.	900 A.D.	1300 yrs.	8
Sophocles	496–406 B.C.	1000 A.D.	1400 yrs.	193
Aristotle	384–322 B.C.	1100 A.D.	1400 yrs.	49 +
Demosthenes	383–322 B.C.	1100 A.D.	1300 yrs.	200
Homer (Illiad)	900 B.C.	400 B.C.	500 yrs.	643
New Testament	48–110 A.D.	125 A.D. (John fragment) 200 A.D. (Bodmer Papyri)	15–90 yrs.	20,000 +

In reference to the above comparison, Metzger writes:

> . . . the work of many an ancient author has been preserved only in manuscripts . . . from the Middle Ages (sometimes the late Middle Ages), far removed from the time at which he lived and wrote. On the contrary, the time between the composition of the books of the New Testament and the earliest extant copies is relatively brief. Instead of the lapse of millenium or more, as in the case of not a few classical authors, several papyrus manu-

scripts of portions of the New Testament are extant which were copied within a century or so after the composition of the original documents. [24]

John Warwick Montgomery writes:

> To express skepticism concerning the resultant text of the New Testament books . . . is to allow all of classical antiquity to slip into obscurity, for no documents of the ancient period are as well attested bibliographically as is the New Testament. [25]

The Internal Evidence Test

This test is best defined in the following quote:

> In this second test, historical and literary scholarship continues to follow Aristotle's dictum that the benefit of the doubt is to be given to the document itself, not arrogated to the critic to himself. This means that one must listen to the claims of the document under analysis, and not assume fraud or error unless the author disqualifies himself by contradictions or known inaccuracies. In the case of the Pauline letters we must give considerable weight to their explicit claim to have been written by the Apostle. In the case of the whole gamut of the New Testament documents we must take seriously when they say, again and again, that they are recording eyewitness testimony or testimony derived from equally reliable sources. [26]

The following excerpts from the New Testament will suffice to demonstrate that the authors wrote as eyewitnesses, or cited firsthand information:

> *Luke 1:1–3*: Many have undertaken to draw up an account of the things that have been fulfilled among us, just as they were handed down to us by those who from the first were eyewitnesses and servants of the word. Therefore, since I myself have carefully investigated everything from the beginning, it seemed good also to me to write an orderly account for you, most excellent Theophilus.

> *2 Pet. 1:16*: We did not follow cleverly invented stories . . . but we were eyewitnesses of his majesty.

> *1 John 1:3*: We proclaim to you what we have seen and heard so that you also may have fellowship with us. And our fellowship is with the Father and with his Son, Jesus Christ.

> *John 19:35*: The man who saw it has given testimony, and his testimony is true. He knows that he tells the truth, and he testifies so that you may also believe.

> *Acts 2:22*: Men of Israel, listen to this: Jesus of Nazareth was a man accredited by God to you by miracles, wonders and signs, which God did among you through him, as you yourselves know.

It is important to note that two of the Gospels—Luke and John—claim directly to have primary-source value. [27] As we shall see in the following section—*The External Evidence Test*—the primary-source value of Matthew and Mark is verified by nonbiblical sources.

F.F. Bruce, former Rylands Professor of Biblical Criticism and Exegesis at the University of Manchester, concerning the New Testament's primary-source value, had this to say:

> The earliest preachers of the gospel knew the value of this first-hand testimony, and appealed to it time and time again, "We are witnesses of these things," was their constant and confident assertion. And it can have been by no means so easy as some writers seem to think to invent words and deeds of Jesus in those early years, when so many of His disciples were about, who could remember what had and had not happened. . . . And it was not only friendly eyewitnesses that the early preachers had to reckon with; there were others less well disposed who were also conversant with the main facts of the ministry and death of Jesus. . . . Had there been any tendency to depart from the facts in any material respect, the possible presence of hostile witnesses in the audience would have served as a further corrective.[28]

To conclude, the internal testimony of the New Testament is that of a document claiming to contain eyewitness testimony of the ministry, death, and resurrection of Jesus of Nazareth.

The External Evidence Test

In this test, the following question is asked:

> Do other historical materials confirm or deny the internal testimony provided by the documents themselves?[29]

Concerning the first century dating of the New Testament, the following extra-biblical writings, which quote passages from the New Testament, support the evidence already presented.

The Epistle of Psuedo-Barnabas (c. A.D. 70–79) contains quotations, and makes many allusions to New Testament books. He cites and alludes to passages from Matthew, and also quotes John 6:51, Rom. 4:11, and 2 Pet. 3:8.[30] It is extremely difficult to quote from nonexistent books.

Corinthians, by Clement of Rome (c. A.D. 95–97) cites passages from Matthew, Mark, Luke, Acts, Titus, 1 Corinthians, Hebrews, 1 Peter, and include a possible allusion to Rev. 22:12.[31] Clement, incidentally, was called by Origen, in *De Principus* (Book II, Chapter 3), a disciple of the apostles (eyewitnesses).[32] Interestingly enough, Clement, who received instruction from the apostles themselves, was thoroughly orthodox in his theology. Therefore, in the case of Clement, his supernatural depiction of Jesus cannot be easily explained away by assuming it to be a product of oral tradition or legend.

The Seven Epistles of Ignatius (c. A.D. 110–117) contain quotations from Matthew, John, Acts, Romans, 1 Corinthians, Ephesians, Philippians, Galatians, Colossians, James, 1 and 2 Thessalonians, 1 and 2 Timothy, and 1 Peter.[33] "St. Ignatius was the third bishop of Antioch, succeeding St. Euodius, who was the immediate successor of St. Peter. Ignatius is considered an Apostolic Father by reason of his having been the hearer of the Apostle John."[34] In light of Ignatius' personal acquaintance with John, it is unlikely that he, like Clement, had a theology which was a product of oral tradition.

Both Ignatius and Clement, who were disciples of the apostles (eyewitnesses), validate the theology contained within the New Testament as being *the* theology of the Church. For example, Ignatius affirms the Deity of Christ,[35] the virgin birth,[36] and the resurrection of Jesus.[37] Clement substantiates the apostles' belief in the resurrection of Christ,[38] and the fact that they taught a general resurrection of all believers.[39] Both these men, being personal acquaintances of the eyewitnesses, successfully demonstrate the primary-source value of the New Testament.

However, this does not exhaust the totality of extra-biblical evidence. Papias, bishop of Hierapolis (c. A.D. 130), writes the following information he received from the Presbyter (Apostle John):

> When Mark became the interpreter of Peter, he wrote down accurately whatever he remembered, though not in order, of the words and deeds of the Lord. . . . Mark, then, made no mistake, but wrote down as he remembered them; and he made it his concern to omit nothing that he had heard nor to falsify anything therein . . . Matthew, indeed, composed the sayings in the Hebrew language; and each one interpreted them to the best of his ability.[40]

Another fine external testimony to the primary-source value of the Gospel accounts is given by Irenaeus, bishop of Lyons, who writes:

> Matthew issued among the Hebrews a written Gospel in their own language, while Peter and Paul were evangelizing in Rome and laying the foundation of the Church. After their departure, Mark, the disciple and interpreter of Peter, also handed down to us in writing what had been preached by Peter. Luke, also the companion of Paul, set down in a book the Gospel preached by him. Afterwards, John, the disciple of the Lord who reclined at His bosom, also published a Gospel, while he was residing in Ephesus in Asia.[41]

Irenaeus' testimony is extremely valuable because he had studied under Polycarp, bishop of Smyrna. Polycarp, who was martyred in A.D. 156, having been a Christian for 86 years, was a disciple of the Apostle John and "always taught what he learned from the apostles."[42] In reference to his relationship with Polycarp, Ireneaus writes:

> I remember the events of those days better than the ones of recent years. . . . I am able to describe the very place in which the blessed Polycarp sat and discoursed. . . and how he spoke of his familiar conversations with John and with the rest of those who had seen the Lord, and how he would recall their words to mind. All that he had heard from them concerning the Lord or about His miracles and about His teachings, having received it from eyewitnesses of the Word of Life, Polycarp related in harmony with the Scriptures.[43]

The external testimonies of Psuedo-Barnabas, Clement, Ignatius, Papias, Polycarp, and Ireneaus validate the first century dating, the primary-source value, and the supernatural Jesus of the New Testament. Further external confirmation of the New Testament's internal testimony, and the historical existence of Jesus, is supplied by the following non-Christian sources.[44]

Cornelius Tacitus, a Roman historian, in A.D. 112, writes of the existence of Roman Christians and of the death of Jesus Christ. He also wrote that Jesus was put to death by Pontius Pilate during the reign of Tiberius (*Annals* XV.44). In a fragment of his *Histories* (Chron.ii.30.6), dealing with the A.D. 70 burning of the Jerusalem temple, Tacitus makes reference to Christianity.

Lucian of Samosta, a second century satirist, spoke only scornful words concerning Jesus and the early Christians. He wrote that the early Christians repudiated polytheism and worshiped Jesus like a god. He also states that Jesus was crucified in Palestine (*The Passing Peregrinus*).

Flavius Josephus, a Jewish historian of the early second century, makes reference to both Christ and the early Christians, and that Christ's disciples believed their Master had risen from the dead. He also wrote that Jesus was crucified under Pilate, and that His ministry, filled with many wonderful works, attracted both Gentile and Jewish followers (*Antiquites* 28.33).

Suetonius, a Roman historian, in A.D. 120, describes the expelling of Christians from Rome and Nero's persecution of the early church (*Life of the Caesars*, 26.2).

Thallus, a Samaritan-born historian, wrote in A.D. 52 that the darkness which fell upon the land during Christ's crucifixion required a naturalistic explanation (a solar eclipse) and was well-known (from the third book of his *Histories*, as cited by Julius Africanus, who argued vigorously against Thallus' interpretation).

Phlegon, a first century historian, also confirms Thallus' affirmation about the darkness which fell upon the land. Phlegon places this during the reign of Tiberius Caesar. Thus, confirming Luke's account (Luke 3:1). (from his *Chronicles*, as cited by Julius Africanus, who cited Phlegon as evidence against Thallus. He is also cited in Origen's *Contra Celsum*, Book 2, sections 14,33,59; and in Philopon's *De. opif. mund. II 21*, concerning the darkness.)

In an A.D. 73 letter (preserved in the British Museum), written by a Syrian named *Mara Bar-Serapian* to his son Serpion, Christ's death is mentioned along with the deaths of Socrates and Pythagores.

Justin Martyr, in his *Defense of Christianity* which he wrote to Emperor Antoninus Pius, refers the emperor to Pilate's report, which Justin supposed was preserved in the imperial archives. In his *Defense*, he cites the *Acts of Pontius Pilate* which according to Justin, records a description of the crucifixion and, in addition, records some of Christ's miracles (*Apology*, 1.48).

Pliny the Younger (c. A.D. 112) wrote an epistle in which he stated that he had killed many Christians while he was governer of Bithynia, and that Christ was worshipped as a god by His disciples. He also wrote that the Christians had a habit of meeting once a week in order to sing hymns to their Lord (*Epistles* X.96).

In addition, the Jewish *Talmud* (Sanhedrin 43a, "Eve of Passover"; and Yeb. IV 3; 49a) acknowledge Christ's existence, but do not look favorably upon His ministry. They attribute His miracles to Satan, His birth to adultery, and acknowledge that He was crucified on the eve of Passover. The Jewish scholars, who would have been more than happy to show that Jesus was a myth, if it were possible, did not believe such an option existed.[45]

The above non-Christian sources confirm the following internal testimony of the New Testament: (1) Jesus was worshipped as God; (2) Jesus performed miracles [though attributed to nontheistic sources]; (3) The disciples of Christ believed that He had risen from the dead; (4) Jesus was crucified under Pontius Pilate in Palestine at Passover time; (5) The sun was darkened on the day of Christ's crucifixion; (6) The early Christians repudiated polytheism; (7) Roman rulers, including Nero, persecuted Christians; (8) The Jewish religious establishment accused Christ of sorcery and of being a bastard; (9) Jesus' ministry occurred under the reign of Tiberius Caesar; and (10) Christ attracted both Jew and Gentile.[46]

New Testament historicity is also confirmed by the findings of archaeology. Because of the abundance of archaeological evidence, we will deal with only four specific discoveries that confirm the New Testament's internal testimony.[47]

The Pavement. According to John 19:13, Jesus was tried by Pilate at a place known as the Pavement. For centuries there had been no record of this place. Fortunately, the Pavement has been recently discovered. Thus, confirming the accuracy of John.[48]

The Pool of Bathesda, which was recorded in no other document except the New Testament, can now be identified with a fair measure of certainty.[49]

The Census, as described in Luke 2:1–3, not recorded outside the New Testament, was assumed to have never occurred. In addition, there was no evidence that Quirinius was governer or that everyone had to return to his own ancestral home. Fortunately, archaeological discoveries show that the Romans held a census every 14 years. They began with Augustus in 23–22 B.C., or 9–8 B.C. The one to which Luke refers would be the latter. Evidence has also been unearthed which verifies that Quirinius was governer of Syria around 7 B.C. A papyrus found in Egypt gives directions for how the census was to be conducted. The procedure concurs with the Lucian account of everyone having to return to his ancestral home.[50]

In Acts 14:6, Luke writes that *Lystra and Derbe* were in Lycaonia and Iconium was not. This, however, is contradicted by the Roman historian Cicero, who indicated that Iconium was in Lycaonia. To the credit of the New Testament, Sir William Ramsey, in 1910, discovered a monument that showed Iconium to be a Phrygian city. This is also confirmed by later discoveries.[51]

Concerning biblical history in the light of archaeological discoveries, Nelson Glueck, renowned Jewish archaeologist, had this to say:

> It may be stated categorically that no archaeological discovery has ever controverted a biblical reference.[52]

It is obvious, from the examination of external sources (extra-biblical writings and archaeological discoveries), that the internal testimony of the New Testament is historically reliable.

Possible Objections

Though we have established that the New Testament is an historically reliable document—in comparison to other ancient literature, beyond a reasonable doubt—most people will still reject the testimony of these documents solely on the basis that it records "miraculous" events. Such a rejection is based only on the assumption that miracles can never happen. But we can only *know* that miracles have never happened if we have no evidence that they have never occurred. If a person assumes that miracles are impossible from the outset, no evidence can convince him. But such a state of mind is closed-minded and unbecoming of any self-respecting skeptic. C.S. Lewis, late Professor of Medieval and Rennaisance Literature at Cambridge University, in response to skeptical philosopher David Hume, reveals the fallacy of this anti-miraculous thinking:

> Now of course, we must agree with Hume that if there is absolutely "uniform experience" against miracles, if in other words they have never happened, why then they never have. Unfortunately, we know the experience against them to be uniform only if we know that all the reports of them are false. And we can know all the reports of them to be false only if we know already that miracles have never occurred. In fact, we are arguing in a circle.[53]

Therefore, the proper question which should be asked, is *not*: "*Can* miracles occur?" But rather: "*Have* miracles occurred?" Since we have demonstrated that the New Testament is a reliable, primary-source recording of the life, death and resurrection of Jesus of Nazareth—a life loaded with miracles—miracles did in fact occur. There is also abundant, reliable evidence available for miracles occurring today.

If, of course, one believes that the disciples of Jesus all got together and concocted the whole thing, one is left with a great psychological absurdity; eleven out of twelve men (John died a natural death) allowed themselves to be martyred for what they knew from the outset was a colossal lie. Having left everything considered precious in the world's eyes—family, social stability, loved ones, religious security—in order to preach that a Jewish carpenter (who they *knew* was dead) had been resurrected and was now sitting at the right hand of God, these men willingly let others put them to death. Having had ample time to recant, they did not. Though it may be argued that many have died for a lie, it is always a lie that is believed to be the truth. However, this is not the case with the disciples of Christ. These men had personal access to His life and knew whether or not their message was true. In light of the fact that the testimony of the disciples could easily stand up in a court of law,[54] it takes an enormous amount of faith to believe the psychological absurdity that they concocted the whole thing, and then went out and died for it.

In addition, it is equally absurd to believe that the disciples were somehow deceived into believing the reality of the resurrection and the miracles of Christ's ministry. Norman L. Geisler, a professor of systematic theology at Dallas Theological Seminary, in reference to this objection, writes the following:

These charges have been made but must be ruled out by the known facts of the case. Mass hallucination or delusion is eliminated by several factors. First, there was the inclination to disbelieve the reports of the resurrection. Hallucination is a phenomenon which occurs when people are already inclined to believe in something. Second, the apostles and eyewitnesses were persons who had known Jesus intimately for years. Recognition was no real problem. Third, there were numerous and independent occasions of long duration, involving conversation and verification by various groups of people, that rule out any possibility of psychological deception. Fourth, mass delusion is ruled out by the numerous independent occasions when one, two, seven, ten, eleven persons had the same experience that the five hundred had. . . . The number and repetition of these miracles rule out any reasonable possibility of delusion.

Since, then, there is no evidence for either individual or collective delusion or hallucination of the eyewitnesses it is necessary to conclude that they were not only honest but also sane witnesses of the events of which they spoke.[55]

Jesus: Deceiver, Deranged, or Deity[56]

Since the New Testament teaches that Jesus claimed to be God (see Chapter 3) and that there is no reason to believe that His disciples knowingly lied about His claims (see above), we have only three choices concerning His character: (a) He was a *deceiver*—He intentionally and knowingly lied about His nature. Therefore, he was not a good man; (b) He was *deranged*—He sincerely believed Himself to be God, but was not. Therefore, He was insane, and a man to be pitied, not emulated; (c) He was *Deity*—He was who He said He was, and should be worshiped. Let us take a look at each possibility.

a. Jesus As Deceiver

The idea of Jesus as a deceiver does not square well with the portrayal of His life in the New Testament. He placed a premium on honesty, love, and righteousness, and despised hypocrisy. The glowing opinions of such non-Christians as philosopher J.S. Mill and historian William Lecky, in addition to the testimony of history itself, repudiate the concept of Christ as a liar.[57]

If Jesus was a deceiver, He let Himself be put to death when He could have recanted prior to His crucifixion. He obviously had ample time to do so (see Matt. 26–27), but chose not to. Therefore, we can only conclude that He sincerely believed Himself to be God Incarnate. If this is the case, He was either God Incarnate or mentally deranged.

b. Jesus As Deranged

If Jesus sincerely thought Himself to be God, and was not God, the conclusion cannot be avoided that He was deranged. Psychiatrists Noyes and Kolb, in their standard medical text, *Modern Clinical Psychiatry*, describe a schizophrenic person as an individual who permits himself to "retreat from the world of reality."[58] If Christ believed Himself to be God and was not, He made a significant "retreat from the world of reality," and therefore must be judged as mentally deranged. But, in light of the profound insight of Christ's moral and ethical precepts, and the New Testament's picture of Christ as a well-balanced individual, can we really doubt His sanity? For this reason, skeptics have been, for the most part, unwilling to declare Christ insane (cf. Mill and Lecky). In fact, psychiatrist J.T. Fisher has written the following psychiatric appraisal of Christ's teachings:

> If you were to take the sum total of all authoritative articles ever written by the most qualified of psychologists and psychiatrists on the subject of mental hygiene—if you were to combine them and refine them and cleave out the excess verbiage—if you were to take the whole of the meat and none of the parsley, and if you were to have these unadulterated bits of pure scientific knowledge concisely expressed by the most capable of living poets, you would have an awkward and incomplete summation of the Sermon on the Mount. And it would suffer immeasurably through comparison. For nearly two thousand years the Christian world has been holding in its hands the complete answer to its restless and fruitless yearnings. Here . . . rests the blueprint for successful human life with optimum mental health and contentment.[59]

If one still insists that Jesus was insane, we have a situation in which one must believe the colossal absurdity that a completely deranged lunatic has given the human race "the blueprint for successful human life with optimum mental health." Who, in their right mind, can accept this conclusion without sacrificing his own sense of reasonableness? As the Catholic apologist, G.K. Chesterton, has written:

> No modern critic in his five wits thinks that the preacher of the Sermon on the Mount was a horrible half-witted imbecile that might be scrawling stars on the walls of a cell. No atheist or blasphemer believes that the author of the Parable of the Prodigal was a monster with one idea like a cyclops with one eye.[60]

Therefore, only one alternative remains.

c. Jesus As Deity

Since He was not a deceiver or deranged, only one option is left: Jesus was who He said He was, namely, God Incarnate.

The Resurrection Verified

From the abundance of all the historical evidence, we believe that we have sufficiently demonstrated the reliability of the New Testament, and have verified the resurrection of Jesus. In light of this, the following quote is most appropriate:

> Out of the first century A.D., when the Resurrection, if untrue, could have been easily disproved by anyone who took the trouble to talk with those who had been present in Jerusalem during the passover week of 33, no contrary

evidence has come; instead, during that century the number of conversions to Christianity increased by geometric progression, the influence of the Gospel story spreading out of Jerusalem like a gigantic web. If Christ did not rise as He promised, how can we rationally explain this lack of negative evidence and number of conversions? Furthermore, if the body of the crucified Jesus naturally left the tomb, how did He leave? Not by its own accord, for Jesus was unquestionably dead. Not through the efforts of the Jewish religious leaders or the Romans, for they had placed a guard at the tomb for the express purpose of keeping the body there. Not Jesus' followers, for to perform such an act would have been to deny the principles of truth upon which their latter lives were predicated and which they preached until killed for their convictions.[61]

It is amazing that even though the works of antiquity do not even begin to approach the reliability of the New Testament, people continue to reject the truth of the resurrection. This rejection is not supported by evidence, but runs contrary to it.

THE AWESOME CONCLUSION

The following is an outline of what our study in this chapter has concluded:

(1) A religious claim, which is true, is one which deals with man's ultimate malady.

(2) Death is this malady.

(3) Jesus claimed to have defeated death in history.

(4) Historical verification operates on the principle of probability. This is not a disadvantage, because in a contingent universe, the certainty of synthetic statements (statements about the world), religious or otherwise, can never rise to 100% proof.

(5) If the New Testament, which contains the account of Jesus' resurrection, can be shown to be historically reliable, then Christ's resurrection can be verified.

(6) According to the three tests of examining the historicity of any document, the New Testament is historically reliable. In addition, to dispense with the New Testament because it contains miracles, as Lewis has observed, is to reason in a circle. Claiming that the disciples (eyewitnesses) made the whole thing up is to ignore the fact that eleven out of twelve of them signed their testimony in blood. And due to their personal access to the events of Christ's ministry, it is equally absurd to believe that they were somehow deceived.

(7) Therefore, Jesus rose from the dead.

From these conclusions, the following are deduced:

(1) Jesus, throughout the Gospels, claimed to be God. He also claimed that His resurrection would verify His Deity.[62]

(2) Jesus rose from the dead, and He is therefore God.

(3) Concerning Christ's character, we have only three choices: deceiver, deranged, or Deity. We have concluded that He could only be Deity.

(4) Thus, we have an excellent reason to put our faith in Jesus Christ. Through a commitment to Christ (putting our faith in Him), the gap between the high probability of the resurrection and the desire for inward certainty is able to be bridged. As Francis Schaeffer once put it: "It should be added in conclusion that the Christian, after he is a Christian, has years of experimental evidence to be added to all the above reasons. . . "[63]

Unlike other religious options, Christianity is not an irrational leap into the darkness of the unverifiable, but rather, a rational and reasoned leap into the light.

And finally, for those who still cling to the popular fallacy that all religions lead to God, and that there are no criteria to judge the truth or falsity of any religion, please accept the following poetic excerpt as a gentle rebuke:

"All roads lead to God,"
I've heard so many people say
But when they get to Jonestown
They beg to look the other way[64]

Chapter 6

CONCLUSION

At the beginning of our study we asked three specific questions concerning the relationship between Baha'ism and Christianity. I believe that our study has sufficiently answered these questions. A careful review will make this point most clear.

First, we asked: Are the teachings of Jesus Christ able to be encompassed into the Baha'i religion without doing any damage to the original intent and meaning of these teachings?

It is safe to say that we can answer no to this question. From our study, we have learned that four chief doctrines of the Christian faith—the Deity of Christ, the bodily resurrection of Christ, the literal Second Coming of Christ, and the uniqueness of Christ's mission—are all denied by the "infallible" spokespersons of the Baha'i religion. The Baha'i faith redefines the original meaning and intent of these doctrines by bending the biblical text.

Second, we asked whether the Baha'i use of the Bible in apologetic matters is successful, compelling or legitimate. We have seen that the Baha'i interpretation of Scripture is indeed illegitimate, due to its lack of proper biblical scholarship. For this reason, it is neither compelling nor successful.

Third, we asked whether the Baha'is have an objective standard, one without bias or prejudice, on which to rest their beliefs, and if Christianity is any different in this respect. The Baha'i religion gives us no compelling reason to believe that Baha'u'llah was telling the truth about himself and God. Apart from a few biblical "prophecies," which we have already demonstrated false, the Baha'is offer no real objective proof that Baha'u'llah is God's manifestation for this age. We have already demonstrated that even the standards that some Baha'i apologists have set up to judge whether an individual is a manifestation have not been fulfilled by some of their alleged manifestations.

On the other hand, we have seen that Christianity rests on the objective proof of the resurrection of Jesus. Jesus, conquering man's greatest foe, has verified His mission and Deity by rising from the dead. The accounts of these events are contained within the documents of the New Testament, which we have seen to be historically reliable.

The Baha'i religion, though containing many theological tenets that appeal to contemporary man, is a faith that is both internally inconsistent and incompatible with Christian belief. For instance, one can literally say that the God of Baha'ism suffers from a cosmic identity crisis. The Baha'i claim that all the major religions teach identical truth is simply not the case. On the nature of God, there is tremendous conflict. Buddha said that it did not matter if God existed or not—Buddha was agnostic. Within Hinduism there are atheistic sects (like Sankhya) and there are sects which believe that God is an impersonal part of everything (like Vedante). Muhammed taught that God was singular and personal. Jesus taught that He Himself is the incarnation of the Second Person of the Triune Godhead. Either one of the religions is right, or they're all wrong. God cannot be everything, nothing, knowable, unknowable, singular, triune, personal, and impersonal all at the same time.

World unity based on the premise that the great religious leaders of history were manifestations of the same God will not lead to unity, but to chaos. For in order to believe this absurdity, one must abandon all rules of logic and sound reasoning. Jesus Christ spoke legitimately when he said, "I am the way and the truth and the life. No one comes to the Father except through me" (John 14:6).

NOTES

Preface

[1]C.E.M. Joad, *Guide To Philosophy* (New York: Dover Publications, 1957), p. 9.

Chapter 1

[1]Shoghi Effendi, *God Passes By* (Wilmette, Ill.: Baha'i Publishing Trust, 1970), p. 3.

[2]Vernon Elvin Johnson, "An Historical Analysis of Critical Transformations in the Evolution of the Baha'i World Faith," Diss. Baylor University 1974, p. 6.

[3]Edward G. Browne, "Babism," *Encyclopedia Britannica*, 11th d., III, pp. 94–95.

[4]These positions are best expounded in 'Abdu'l-Baha', *Some Answered Questions*, trans. Laura Clifford Barney (Wilmette, Ill.: Baha'i Publishing Trust, 1930).

[5]Alessandro Bausani, "The Religious Crises of the Modern World," *World Order*, 2, No. 3 (1968): 13.

[6]'Abdu'l-Baha', *The Promulgation of Universal Peace* (Wilmette, Ill.: Baha'i Publishing Trust, 1982), p. 346; and George Townshend, *Promise of All Ages* (Wilmette, Ill.: Baha'i Publishing Trust, 1948), pp. 1–127.

[7]Johnson, op. cit. pp. 5–6.

[8]The basic outline for the following historical scenario is taken from Lewis M. Hopfe, *Religions of the World* (Encino, Calif.: Glencoe Publishing Co., 1979), pp. 353–355.

[9]Ibid., p. 353.

[10]Effendi, *God*, pp. 3–85.

[11]Seyyed 'Ali Mohammed dit le Bab, *Le Beyan Persan*, traduit du Persan par A.-L.-M. Nicolas, 4 vols. (Paris: Librairie Paul Geuthner, 1911–1914), VIII, 10, as cited in Johnson, p. 160. Remaining references to *Le Beyan Persan*, in this chapter, will be in the text.

[12]Ibid.

[13]Ibid., p. 158.

[14]Ibid.

[15]Ibid., p. 159.

[16]Effendi, *God*, pp. 3–85.

[17]Ibid., pp. 89–150.

[18]Ibid.

[19]Ibid., pp. 151–182.

[20]Ibid., pp. 163–220.

[21]Shoghi Effendi, *The World Order of Baha'u'llah* (Wilmette, Ill.: Baha'i Publishing Trust, 1955), p. 133.

[22]Effendi, *God*, pp. 221–234.

[23]Ibid., pp. 235–309.

[24]Ibid., pp. 321–401; and Gloria Faizi, *The Baha'i Faith: An Introduction* (n.p., 1971), pp. 87–116.

[25]Johnson, op. cit. pp. 362–380.

[26]See Glenford Mitchell, "The Assault Upon Iran's Baha'is (Statement of National Spiritual Assembly of Baha'is in Iran," *World Order*, 16, No. 3 (1982): 31–33.

Chapter 2

[1]'Abdu'l-Baha', *Questions*, p. 168.

[2]Baha'u'llah, *Gleanings From the Writings of Baha'u'llah*, trans. Shoghi Effendi (Wilmette, Ill.: Baha'i Publishing Trust, 1939), pp. 46–47.

[3]'Abdu'l-Baha', *Questions*, pp. 168–169.

[4]Ibid., p. 169.

[5]Ibid.

[6]Baha'u'llah, *Gleanings*, p. 48.

[7]Shoghi Effendi, *Call To the Nations* (Chatham, Great Britain: W&J Mackay Limited, 1977), p. xi.

[8]Townshend, *Promise*, pp. 51–52.

[9]Ibid.

[10]Ibid., p. 52.

[11]Faizi, p. 34.

[12]Townshend, *Promise*, pp. 52–53.

[13]'Abdu'l-Baha' and Baha'u'llah, *Baha'i World Faith* (Wilmette, Ill.: Baha'i Publishing Trust, 1956), p. 21.

[14]Townshend, *Promise*, p. 47.

[15]Ibid.

[16]Ibid., p. 49.

[17]Ibid.

[18]'Abdu'l-Baha', *Questions*, p. 195.

[19]Faizi, op. cit. p. 28.

[20]Townshend, *Promise*, p. 50.

[21]Ibid., p. 51.

[22]Ibid.

[23]'Abdu'l-Baha', *Questions*, p. 189.

[24]'Abdu'l-Baha', *Universal Peace*, p. 346.

[25]Seyyed Ali Mohammed dit le Bab, III, 3, as cited in Johnson, p. 154.

[26]Hud, an ancient Arabian prophet after whom the eleventh surah of the Qur'an is named, according to the Qur'an, was sent to his people of the tribe of A'ad (See Qur'an VII,65; XI,50; XXVI,124; XCVI,21).

[27]Salih, sent to the tribe of Thamud, was another Arabian prophet (See Qur'an VII,75; XI,61; XXVI,142; XXVII,45).

[28]Baha'u'llah, *The Kitab-i-Iqan: The Book of Certitude*, 2nd. ed., trans. Shoghi Effendi (Wilmette, Ill.: Baha'i Publishing Trust, 1950), pp. 7–65.

[29]*One Universal Faith* (Wilmette, Ill.: Baha'i Publishing Trust, n.d.), p. 5.

[30]Hugh E. Chance, "Baha'i Faith," *Collier's Encyclopedia*, 1965, III, 462.

[31]Baha'u'llah, *Gleanings*, p. 49.

[32]'Abdu'l-Baha', *Questions*, pp. 129–130.

[33]Ibid., p. 97.

[34]Ibid., p. 169.

[35]Baha'u'llah, *Gleanings*, p. 49.

[36]Townshend, *Promise*, pp. 61–63.

[37]These passages will be presented in chapter 4.

[38]'Abdu'l-Baha', *Questions*, p. 127.

[39]Ibid., pp. 119–120.

[40]Ibid., pp. 120–121.

[41]Townshend, *Promise*, p. 43.

[42]Ibid., p. 40.

Chapter 3

[1]*The Bhagavad Gita*, trans. Juan Mascaro (Harmondsworth, Middlesex: Penguin Books, 1962), 3:11a,12a.

[2]Ibid., 13:15, 16, 30.

[3]Ibid., 10:21.

[4]L.H. Mill, *Sacred Books of the East*, 31:195–196, as quoted in Robert Ernest Hume, *The World's Living Religions* (New York: Charles Scribner's Sons, 1924), p. 202.

[5]Ibid., 203.

[6]Ibid., 10:21.

[7]Ward Fellows, *Religions East and West* (New York: Holt, Rinehart, and Winston, 1979), p. 147.

[8]Ibid., pp. 138–152.

[9]Hopfe, op. cit. p. 183.

[10]Hume, op. cit. pp. 223–225.

[11]Effendi, *Call*, p. xi.

[12]Townshend, *Promise*, pp. 51–52.

[13]Ibid., p. 49.

[14]Josh McDowell and Don Stewart, *Answers To Tough Questions* (San Bernardino, Calif.: Here's Life Publishers, 1980), p. 19.

[15]Analects 2:4.1, as quoted in Hume, op. cit. p. 110.

[16]Analects 7:17, 24, 31; 8:3.1–3; 16:13.1–3; 17:9.1–7, as noted in Ibid., p.111.

[17]'Abdu'l-Baha', *Questions*, p. 195.

[18]Hume, op. cit. p. 113.

[19]As quoted in Ibid.

[20]As quoted and noted in Ibid.

[21]*The Meaning of the Glorious Koran*, trans. Mohammed Marmaduke Pickthall (New York: Mentor Books, n.d.), p. 365.

[22]'Abdu'l-Baha', *Questions*, p. 195.

[23]*The Altizer-Montgomery Dialogue* (Chicago: Inter-Varsity Press, 1967), p. 21.

[24]Townshend, *Promise*, p. 50.

[25]Effendi, *Call*, p. xi.

[26]Faizi, op. cit. p. 33.

[27]See Josh McDowell, *Evidence That Demands a Verdict*, rev. ed. (San Bernardino, Calif.: Here's Life Publishers, 1979); and chapter 5 of this book.

[28]Baha'u'llah, *Gleanings*, p. 49.

[29]Ibid., p. 48.

[30]List compiled by Walter R. Martin, *Kingdom of the Cults*, rev. ed. (Minneapolis: Bethany House Publishers, 1985), p. 87–88.

[31]Ibid.

[32]*The Greek New Testament*, ed. Kurt Aland, Matthew Black, Carlo M. Martini, Bruce M. Metzger, and Allen Wikgren, 3rd ed. (West Germany: United Bible Societies, 1983), p. 363.

[33]Martin, op. cit. p. 78.

[34]Other Scriptural references that verify Christ's Deity can be found in Ibid., pp. 73–86.

[35]Baha'u'llah, *Gleanings*, p. 54.

[36]Ibid.

[37]'Abdu'l-Baha', *Questions*, pp. 127–128.

[38]Townshend, *God*, Intro., p. ix.

[39]Townshend, *Promise*, p. 67; and 'Abdu'l-Baha', *Questions*, p. 128.

[40]Townshend, *Promise*, p. 67.

[41]"At the first coming he came from heaven, though apparently from the womb; in the same way also, at his second coming, he will come from heaven, though apparently from the womb." ('Abdu'l-Baha', *Questions*, p. 127)

[42]These will presented and critiqued in chapter 4.

[43]*The Greek New Testament*, op. cit. pp. 79, 837.

[44]'Abdu'l-Baha', *Questions*, pp. 120–121.

[45]Ibid., p. 117.

[46]Joseph Henry Thayer, *Greek-English Lexicon of the New Testament* (Grand Rapids, Mich.: Zondervan, 1979), p. 611.

[47]This argument was given on a recent program of the *John Ankerberg Show* by two Baha'is who were debating Walter R. Martin. In reference to this argument, Townshend translates Matthew 28:20b as: "I am with you always even to the end of the *dispensation*." (Townshend, *Promise*, p. 63)

[48]*The Greek New Testament*, op. cit. p. 92, 117.

Chapter 4

[1]'Abdu'l-Baha', *Questions*, p. 44.

[2]Ibid., p. 30.

[3]Ibid., p. 48.

[4]Robert D. Culver, "Daniel," in *The Wycliffe Bible Commentary* , ed. Charles F. Pfeiffer and Everett F. Harrison (Chicago: Moody Press, 1962), p. 793.

[5]Charles Lee Feinberg, *Daniel: The Man and His Visions* (Chappaqua, N.Y.: Christian Herald Books, 1981), p. 107.

[6]McDowell, op. cit. pp. 172–173.

[7]Ibid., p. 173. In order to arrive at the proper date, we multiply 360 days $\times$ 2,300 "years," which equals 828,000 days. These 828,000 days are in turn divided by a solar year, 365.24219879 days, equalling approximately 2267 solar years. Adding the 2267 years to 444 B.C. we arrive at 1823 A.D. Thus 'Abdu'l-Baha' is way off the mark.

[8]'Abdu'l-Baha', *Questions*, p. 48.

[9]McDowell, op. cit. p. 173.

[10]'Abdu'l-Baha', *Questions*, p. 73.

[11]Ibid.

[12]Ibid., p. 76.

[13]Elisabeth H. Cheney, *Prophecy Fulfilled* (Wilmette, Ill.: Baha'i Publishing Trust, 1972), p. 16.

[14]Ibid., pp. 16–17.

[15]Ibid., p. 13.

[16]Ibid.

[17]Ibid., p. 14.

[18]Ibid., pp. 14–15.

[19]Ibid., p. 15.

[20]Ibid., pp. 14–15.

[21]Ibid.

[22]Gleason Archer, "Isaiah," in *Wycliffe*, p. 49.

[23]Gleason Archer, *Encyclopedia of Bible Difficulties* (Grand Rapids, Mich.: Zondervan, 1982), p. 268.

[24]J.E. Esslemont, *Baha'u'llah and the New Era* (New York: Baha'i Publishing Committee, 1923), p. 278.

[25]Ibid., pp. 288–289.

[26]J.E. Esslemont, *Baha'u'llah and the New Era*, 3rd ed. (Wilmette, Ill.: Baha'i Publishing Trust, 1970), pp. 249–250.

Chapter 5

[1]John Warwick Montgomery, *Faith Founded On Fact* (New York: Thomas Nelson, 1978), p. 120.

[2]Edward John Carnell, *An Introduction To Christian Apologetics* (Grand Rapids, Mich.: Eerdman's Publishing, 1948), pp. 24–25.

[3]Albert Camus, "Absurd Walls," in *Phenomonology and Existentialism*, ed. Robert C. Solomon (Lathan, Mary.: University Press of America, Inc., 1980), pp. 490–491.

[4]Ibid., p. 491.

[5]John 11:23–24.

[6]1 Corinthians 15:1–8.

[7]John 19:35.

[8]Papias said: "When Mark became the interpreter of Peter, he wrote down accurately whatever he remembered . . . Mark then made no mistake . . ." (Papias, "Explanations of the Sayings of the Lord," in *Faith of the Early Fathers*, ed. William A. Jurgens [Collegeville, Minn.: The Liturgical Press, 1970], p. 39) Papias was a disciple of the Apostle John.

[9]Luke 1:1–3.

[10]Hans Hahn, "Logic, Mathematics and Knowledge of Nature," in *20th Century Philosophy: The Analytic Tradition*, ed. Morris Weitz (New York: The Free Press, 1966), p. 230.

[11]McDowell, op. cit. p. 39.

[12]C. Sanders, *Introduction in Research in English Literary History* (New York: Macmillan, 1952), p. 143ff.

[13]McDowell, op. cit. p. 39.

[14]Norman L. Geisler and William Nix, *A General Introduction To the Bible* (Chicago: Moody Press, 1968), p. 267.

[15]The following list of manuscripts is taken from Norman L. Geisler, *Christian Apologetics* (Grand Rapids, Mich.: Baker Book House, 1976), pp. 306–307.

[16]Bruce M. Metzger, *The Text of the New Testament* (New York: Oxford University Press, 1968), p. 39.

[17]Geisler, op. cit. p. 306.

[18]Metzger, op. cit. pp. 31–33.

[19]Ibid., pp. 40, 48–50

[20]See Donald Guthrie, *New Testament Introduction* (Downers Grove, Ill.: Inter-Varsity Press, 1970), pp. 45–46, 72–76, 113, 282–283, 346; and F.F. Bruce, *The New Testament Documents: Are They Reliable?* (Downers Grove, Ill.: Inter-Varsity Press, 1980), pp. 13–14.

[21]Richard Riss, *Evidence For the Resurrection of Jesus Christ* (Minneapolis: Bethany House Publishers, 1977), pp. 20–21.

[22]William F. Albright interview in *Christianity Today*, Jan. 18, 1963, as quoted in McDowell, p. 63.

[23]For confirmation of this list see F.W. Hall, "Manuscript Authorities For the Text of the Chief Classical Writers," in *Companion To Classical Text* (Oxford: Clarendon Press, 1913), pp. 199ff.

[24]Metzger, op. cit. pp. 34–35.

[25]John Warwick Montgomery, *Where Is History Going?* (Minneapolis: Bethany House Publishers, 1969), p. 46.

[26]John Warwick Montgomery, *History and Christianity* (Downers Grove, Ill.: Inter-Varsity Press, 1964), pp. 29–30.

[27]However, concerning Mark, the following quote is most helpful: "C.H. Turner pointed out that Mark's Gospel reflects an eyewitness account of many scenes, for when the third person plural passes on to a third person singular involving Peter, we have the indirect equivalent of first person direct discourse, deriving from the Apostle." (Ibid., p. 31)

[28]F.F. Bruce, *The New Testament Documents*, pp. 45–46.

[29]Montgomery, *Christianity*, p. 31.

[30]Geisler and Nix, op. cit. p. 348.

[31]Ibid.

[32]McDowell, op. cit. p. 51. This is also substantiated by the Early Church Father, Tertullian, who said: ". . . Clement was ordained by Peter. . ." (Tertullian, "Demurrer Against the Heretics," in *Early Fathers*, p. 122).

[33]Geisler and Nix, op. cit. pp. 348–349.

[34]William Jurgens, "St. Ignatius of Antioch," in *Early Fathers*, p. 17.

[35]Ignatius, "Letter to the Ephesians," in *Early Fathers*, pp. 17–18.

[36]Ibid., p. 18.

[37]Ignatius, "Letter to the Trallians," in *Early Fathers*, p. 21.

[38]Clement, "Letter to the Corinthians," in *Early Fathers*, p. 8.

[39]Ibid., p. 9.

[40]Papias, p. 39. This writing of Papias is preserved in the writings of the Church historian, Eusebius. ("History of the Church," in *Early Fathers*, pp. 38–39).

[41]Irenaeus, "Against Heretics," in *Early Fathers*, p. 89.

[42]Ibid., p. 90.

[43]In Eusebius, op. cit. p. 106.

[44]The following sources are documented in McDowell, pp. 81–84; and Bruce, pp. 113–115.

[45]See Joseph Klausner, *Jesus of Nazareth* (New York: Macmillan, 1925), pp. 23–28. Klausner, a Jewish scholar, documents many citations from the *Talmud* that verify Christ's historicity.

[46]A similar list is found in Geisler, op. cit. p. 325.

[47]For a more complete list of archaeological confirmation of New Testament historicity see McDowell, op. cit. pp. 70–73.

[48]William F. Albright, *The Archaeology of Palestine*, rev. ed. (Harmondsworth, Middlesex: Pelican Books, 1960), p. 141.

[49]F.F. Bruce, "Archaeological Confirmation of the New Testament," in *Revelation and the Bible*, ed. Carl F.H. Henry (Grand Rapids, Mich.: Baker Book House, 1969), p. 329.

[50]John Elder, *Prophets, Idols, and Diggers* (New York: Bobbs-Merrill, 1960), pp. 159–160; and Joseph Free, *Archaeology and Bible History* (Wheaton, Ill.: Scripture Press Publications, 1969), p. 285.

[51]Free, p. 317.

[52]Nelson Glueck, *Rivers in the Desert; History of Nageu* (Philadelphia: Jewish Publications Society of America, 1969), p. 31.

[53]C.S. Lewis, *Miracles* (New York: Macmillan, 1947), p. 105.

[54]Simon Greenleaf (1783–1853), famous Royal Professor of Law at Harvard University, whose efforts, along with that of Justice Joseph Story, "ascribed the rise of the Harvard Law School to its eminent position among the legal schools of the United States" (H.W.H. Knott, in *Dictionary of American Biography*, Vol. 8 [New York, 1937], p. 584), wrote the famous *A Treatise on the Law of Evidence* (1842), which was "regarded as the foremost American authority." Applying the law of evidence to the Gospel accounts, Greenleaf wrote *An Examination of the Testimony of the Four Evangelists by the Rules of Evidence Administered in the Courts of Justice* (1846). (This book is reprinted in John Warwick Montgomery, *The Law Above the Law* [Minneapolis: Bethany House Publishers, 1975]) Professor J.N.D. Anderson, former Director of the Institute of Advanced Legal Studies in the University of London and a world-renowned expert in Muslim law, has written *Christianity: The Witness of History* (London: Tyndale Press, 1969), and *The Evidence for the Resurrection* (London: Inter-Varsity Fellowship, 1966). See also Thomas Sherlock, Master of the Temple, *Tryal of the Witnesses* (1729), as reprinted in *Jurisprudence: A Book of Readings*, 2nd ed., ed. John Warwick Montgomery (Strasbourg, France: International Scholarly Publishers; Orange, Calif.: The Simon Greenleaf School of Law, 1980).

[55]Geisler, op. cit. p. 316.

[56]Similar presentations are found in; Peter Kreeft, *Between Heaven and Hell* (Downers Grove, Ill.: Inter-Varsity Press, 1982); C.S. Lewis, *Mere Christianity* (New York: Macmillan, 1958); McDowell, op. cit.; and Montgomery, *Christianity*.

[57]Mill writes that Christ was ". . .the greatest moral reformer and martyr to that mission who ever existed on earth. . ." (As quoted in Vernon C. Grounds, *The Reason For Our Hope* [Chicago: Moody Press, 1945], p. 34). Lecky writes that Christ has given the world ". . . not only the highest pattern of virtue, but the strongest incentive to its practice. . ." (William E. Lecky, *History of European Morals From Augustus to Charlemagne*, 2nd ed. [London: Longmans, Green, 1869], II: 88).

[58]*Modern Clinical Psychiatry* (Philadelphia and London: Saunders, 1958), p. 401, as quoted in Montgomery, *Christianity*, p. 64.

[59]J.T. Fisher and L.S. Hawley, *A Few Buttons Missing* (Philadelphia: J.B. Lippincott, 1951), p. 273, as quoted in Montgomery, *Christianity*, p. 65.

[60]G.K. Chesterton, *The Everlasting Man* (Garden City, N.J.: Image Books, 1955), pp. 201–202.

[61]John Warwick Montgomery, "The Quest For Absolutes: An Historical Argument," unpublished mimeograph, p. 7.

[62]John 8:58 cf. Exodus 3:14. In Mark 2:1–12, Jesus forgives sins. See also chapter 3 of this present work. Jesus states that the resurrection will verify His Deity in John 2:18–21.

[63]Francis A. Schaeffer, *The God Who Is There* (Downers Grove, Ill.: Inter-Varsity Press, 1968), p. 111.

[64]Excerpt from Francis J. Beckwith, "Illusion of Technique," unpublished poem (1982).

SUGGESTED BIBLIOGRAPHY

Works By Baha'i Authors

'Abdu'l-Baha'. *Some Answered Questions*. Translated by Laura Clifford Barney. Wilmette, Ill.: Baha'i Publishing Trust, 1930.

'Abdu'l-Baha' and Baha'u'llah. *Baha'i World Faith*. Wilmette, Ill.: Baha'i Publishing Trust, 1956.

Cheney, Elisabeth. *Prophecy Fulfilled*. Wilmette, Ill.: Baha'i Publishing Trust, 1972.

Effendi, Shoghi. *Call To the Nations*. Chatam, Great Britain: W&J Mackay Limited, 1977.

_____. *God Passes By*. Willmette, Ill.: Baha'i Publishing Trust, 1970.

Esslemont, J.E. *Baha'u'llah and the New Era*. 3rd ed. Wilmette, Ill.: Baha'i Publishing Trust, 1970.

Faizi, Gloria. *The Baha'i Faith: An Introduction*. n.p., 1971.

Townshend, George. *The Heart of the Gospel or the Bible and the Baha'i Faith*. Oxford: George Roland, 1951.

_____. *Promise of All Ages*. Wilmette, Ill.: Baha'i Publishing Trust, 1974.

Works by Non-Baha'i Authors

Beckwith, Francis J. "Baha'ism: A Presentation and Critique of Its Theological Tenets and Apologetic Use of the Christian Scriptures." M.A. Thesis Simon Greenleaf School of Law, 1984. This can be obtained through the Theological Research Exchange Network (TREN) from the Microfilm Service Company of Portland, Oregon.

Boykin, John. *The Baha'i Faith*. Downers Grove, Ill.: Inter-Varsity Press, 1982.

Martin, Walter R. *The Kingdom of the Cults*. 3rd ed. Minneapolis: Bethany House Publishers, 1985.

Miller, William McElwee. *The Baha'i Faith: Its History and Teachings*. South Pasadena, Calif.: William Carey Library, 1974.

Richards, John R. *The Religion of the Baha'is*. London: Society Promoting Christian Knowledge, 1932.

Wilson, Samuel Graham. *Baha'ism and Its Claims*. New York: Fleming H. Revell, 1915.